Chronology

SOME PRINCIPAL EVENTS IN ROMAN MILITARY HISTORY, FROM THE DEATH OF CAESAR TO THE REIGN OF TRAJAN.

44 BC: Conspirators assassinate the Dictator, Gaius **Julius Caesar**. Marcus Antonius, a close friend of Caesar, takes control and inflames public opinion against the conspirators, forcing Brutus and Cassius, the prime movers, to flee Italy.

The great-nephew of the Dictator, Gaius Julius Caesar Octavianus, succeeds in gaining the support of the Senate against Antonius and emerges as his rival for power.

43 BC: Octavianus defeats Antonius at Mutina and the latter retreats across the Alps to Gallia Narbonensis. Octavianus becomes reconciled with Antonius later in the year, and together with Marcus Aemilius Lepidus, who replaced Caesar as chief priest, they form the Second Triumvirate[1].

42 BC: Octavianus and Antonius engage and defeat Brutus and Cassius at Philippi in Macedonia. Both conspirators commit suicide.

40 BC: Octavianus and Antonius agree to divide the rule of the Roman world between them and Antonius marries Octavia, the sister of Octavianus.

36 BC: Antonius campaigns against the Parthians.

33 BC: Mistrust and rivalry between the two leaders worsens, largely as a result of Antonius' association with the Egyptian queen, Cleopatra.

32 BC: Antonius formally divorces Octavia in favour of Cleopatra, and the breech between the two leaders becomes irreconcilable.

The grave stele of Caius Valerius Crispus, a legionary of Legio VIII Augusta, who served during the first half of the 1st century AD—see colour plate C1. (In the collection of the Stadtisches Museum, Wiesbaden)

[1]An officially constituted dictatorial committee.

3

31 BC:	Antonius and Cleopatra are defeated in a naval engagement off Actium and retreat to Egypt.
30 BC:	Octavianus takes Egypt and both Antonius and Cleopatra commit suicide. Octavianus becomes the effective ruler of the Roman world.
27 BC:	Octavianus takes the titles 'Imperator' and '**Augustus**', and becomes the first Roman Emperor.
25 BC:	Galatia is annexed as a Roman province.
16–15 BC:	Tiberius and Nero Drusus, stepsons of Augustus, annexe the provinces of Noricum and Raetia.
12–9 BC:	The territory north of Illyricum is annexed by Tiberius as the province of Pannonia.

Birth of Christ

AD 9:	Three legions under P. Quinctilius Varus—the XVIIth, XVIIIth and XIXth—are destroyed in the Teutoburg Forest: an extremely serious loss of men and equipment which forestalls Roman intentions of annexation across the Rhine.
AD 14:	Augustus dies and the Rhine and Pannonian legions mutiny. His successor, **Tiberius** Cladius Nero, quells the revolt and army conditions are improved to avoid further trouble.
AD 14–16:	Germanicus undertakes three campaigns against the Germans east of the Rhine and reaches the River Elbe, but no permanent presence is established.
AD 37:	Tiberius dies and is succeeded by the insane Gaius Caesar, nicknamed '**Caligula**'. Gaius Caesar may have been a victim of lead poisoning.[1]
AD 41:	Gaius Caesar is assassinated by officers of the Praetorian Guard at the age of 29 and is succeeded by Tiberius **Claudius** Drusus.
AD 43:	Four legions invade Britain under the command of Aulus Plautius. Claudius briefly visits the new province.

[1]*Decline and Fall: Were the Romans Poisoned?* Peter Cooper, FPS, The Pharmaceutical Journal, December 22 and 29, 1973.

AD 54:	Claudius dies, probably poisoned by his second wife, Agrippina the Younger, who secures the succession for her son **Nero** Claudius Caesar Drusus Germanicus, who assassinates her in AD 59.
AD 60:	The Druids and other anti-Roman elements on Mona Insulis (Anglesey) are massacred by Suetonius Paulinus; this operation is followed immediately by a serious revolt in south-east Britain, led by the implacable Icenian Queen Boudica.
AD 61:	Paulinus crushes the Boudican Revolt.
AD 64:	A large area of the city of Rome is destroyed by fire. The Christian sect is blamed initially, but the Emperor himself is suspected latterly of deliberately firing the city to make way for the construction of his Golden House.
AD 66:	A major revolt breaks out in Judaea; Vespasianus is sent to restore order.
AD 68:	Julius Vindex, Governor of Central Gaul revolts against Nero, but is killed at the battle of Vesontio (Besançon). The aging Sulpicius **Galba**, Governor of Nearer Spain, revolts also and is supported by the Senate. He marches on Rome, and Nero commits suicide.
AD 69:	The Year of the Three Caesars. Galba becomes unpopular and earns the particular displeasure of Marcus Salvius **Otho** by not choosing him as his successor. Otho arranges Galba's murder and succeeds with the support of a large number of legions. However, Aulus **Vitellius** is hailed Emperor by the Rhine legions and marches on Rome. He defeats Otho at the first battle of Bedriacum, near Cremona, and Otho commits suicide. Vitellius succeeds, only to learn that the eastern legions have declared for their general Vespasianus. The forces of Vitellius are defeated by the pro-Vespasianus general Primus at the second battle of Bedriacum. Flavius Sabinus **Vespasianus** succeeds and the civil war closes.

FVNDATORIQVIETIS

A section of the triumphal relief from Trajan's Forum, later incorporated into the Arch of Constantine. The sculpture shows cavalry wearing mail and scale body defences, and legionary infantry wearing cuirasses with laminations on the breast instead of breast-plates. (Trajan's Column, Rome)

AD 70: The city of Jerusalem falls to the besieging Roman force under the command of Vespasianus' son Titus. General Flavius Silva is sent to invest the Herodian fortress of Masada, which has been occupied by a band of Sicarii and others of the anti-Roman faction.

AD 73: Masada falls. The besieged Jews commit suicide rather than surrender to the Romans.

AD 79: Vespasianus dies after a stable reign and is succeeded by his son **Titus**.

AD 81: Titus dies prematurely at the age of 42, having completed the building of the great Flavian amphitheatre at Rome, known today as the Colosseum, begun by his father in AD 72. Titus is succeeded by his younger brother, Titus Flavius **Domitianus**. (Rumours that Domitianus was responsible for Titus' early death were never proven; however, Domitianus was an unpleasant character and was doubtless bitterly jealous of his popular brother.)

AD 89: Antonius Saturninus, Governor of Upper Germany, revolts against Domitianus, but is brought to battle and defeated on the plain of Andernach by Maximus, the Governor of Lower Germany.

AD 96: Domitianus is finally murdered, bringing the Flavian Dynasty to an end. He is succeeded by Marcus Cocceius **Nerva**.

AD 98: Nerva dies having adopted the 44-year-old Governor of Upper Germany, Marcus Ulpius **Trajanus**, as his successor—a most fortunate choice. Trajanus proves to be an excellent soldier and a statesman, a rare combination. Considered to be the finest Roman Emperor, he extends the Empire to its largest geographical size.

Introduction

'Had previous chroniclers neglected to speak in praise of History in general, it might perhaps have been necessary for me to recommend everyone to choose for study and welcome such treatises as the present, since man has no more ready corrective of conduct than knowledge of the past. . . For who is so worthless or indolent as not to wish to know by what means and under what system of polity the Romans in less than 53 years have succeeded in subjecting nearly the whole inhabited world to their sole government, a thing unique in history?' (Polybius)

Probably the most fruitful of the Romans for such study are their soldiers—men of great courage, determination and ability, whose faces still stare silently out at us with an air of grave dignity from sculptures once bright with paint and bronze ornament.

Though the common soldiers have left no known written account of their experiences, the earth has yielded large quantities of objects in varying states of preservation, which have enabled modern man to learn much of the life of the ancient soldier. Literature, too, has survived from antiquity, providing us with valuable clues and even direct and accurate descriptions of military equipment, which are increasingly being verified by archaeological finds.

Quite detailed information has also been derived from sculptural works, the foremost of these being the great column erected in the early second century AD by the Emperor Marcus Ulpius Trajanus to commemorate his victories over the Dacians. We can still see, spiralling up this 132-foot monument, the army of Trajan performing the various deeds of the campaign and going about their multitude of military tasks. This has, of course, proved to be of inestimable value to historians not only from the aspect of military equipment, but also with regard to the appearance of forts and bridges of a more temporary nature of which little or nothing survives. The partial reconstruction of a turf and timber rampart and gate in its original position at the Lunt Fort, Baginton, near Coventry is largely based upon information derived from this monument.

While Trajan's Column (a two-part cast of which may be seen in the Victoria and Albert Museum, London) has proved to contain some surprisingly accurate details of Roman military practice, it must still be treated with a great deal of caution, especially with regard to the proportions of certain objects such as shields; these are invariably shown on a reduced scale. A similar concession was made to aesthetics by narrowing the cheek-guards of helmets in order that the faces of the men would become more visible. This vast work, which was no doubt painted originally, like so many other ancient sculptures, would also have bristled with bronze weapons where now there are only empty hands; the bronze has long since vanished into the crucibles of later ages.

The Composition of the Army

The Roman military of this period may be divided into two distinct parts, the legions and the auxilia, with a marked social division between them.

The ranks of a legion were entirely filled by Roman citizens. This does not mean that they were all men of Italian origin, but that the individual, be he a Gaul, Iberian, or whatever, possessed the coveted 'citizenship', which was hereditary—for example, it will be recalled that the father of Saul of Tarsus was granted the citizenship for services to the Roman army in the capacity of tentmaker. This would have meant that, had he possessed the required mental and physical development, the young Saul would have been eligible for service with a legion. As we know, he did make use of one of

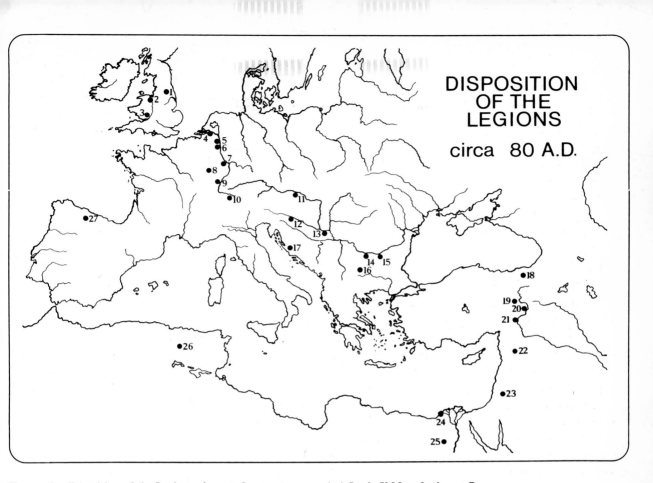

DISPOSITION OF THE LEGIONS
circa 80 A.D.

Key to the disposition of the Legions circa AD 80:

(1) Legio IX Hispana at York.
(2) Legiones XX Valeria and II Adiutrix at Chester.
(3) Legio II Augusta at Caerleon.
(4) Legiones XXII Primigenia and X Gemina at Nijmegen.
(5) Legio VI Victrix at Neuss.
(6) Legio XXI Rapax at Bonn.
(7) Legio XIV Gemina at Mainz.
(8) Legio I Adiutrix at or near Mainz.
(9) Legio VIII Augusta at Strasbourg.
(10) Legio XI Claudia at Windish.
(11) Legio XV Apollinaris at Carnuntum.
(12) Legio XIII Gemina at Poetovio.
(13) Legio VII Claudia at Viminiacum.
(14) Legio V Macedonica at Oescus.
(15) Legio I Italica at Novae.
(16) Legio V Alaudae on or near the Danube.
(17) Legio IV Flavia Firma at Burnum.
(18) Legio XVI Flavia Firma at Satala.
(19) Legio XII Fulminata at Melitene.
(20) Legio VI Ferrata at Samosata.
(21) Legio IV Sythica at Cyrrhus.
(22) Legio III Gallica at Danabe near Damascus.
(23) Legio X Fretensis at Jerusalem.
(24) Legio XXII Deiotariana at Alexandria.
(25) Legio III Cyrenaica at Coptos near Luxor.
(26) Legio III Augusta at Ammaedara near Tebessa.
(27) Legio VII Gemina at Leon.

the rights bestowed by his citizenship, in that he made legal appeal to the very head of the Roman State, the Emperor himself.

A large number of the legionary soldiers were skilled tradesmen. Skills which would be acquired during the early years of their service enabled the men to increase their rates of pay and to be promoted to the rank of *immunis*. No doubt this rank excused them from such necessary but irksome tasks as latrine duty. The presence of these skilled men within the ranks rendered a legion, as far as possible, a self-sufficient unit, which could provide its own forts and fortifications and other structures, such as bridges and war machinery. Since the men were being trained almost wholly as military engineers and professional killers, it is hardly surprising that one seldom encounters a well-lettered inscription or artistic relief that was the product of their hands. Such things require a great deal of aptitude and experience, and when accomplished works of the kind are found in a military context they are more likely to be the efforts of civilians employed specifically for such purposes.

The legions were supported by the non-citizen *auxilia*, which in Caesar's time was not a regular arm of the Roman forces and therefore did not

A section of a relief at Rome showing Praetorian guards carrying javelins with lead (or possibly cast bronze) loads, and long shields of the late Republic, which had become a traditional part of their equipment by the 1st century AD when this relief was carved. (The Cancelleria Relief, in the collection of the Vatican Museum)

surviving bronze diploma refers to the honourable discharge before expiration of service of an entire *Cohors Equitata*—the *Ulpia Torquata*, which was raised in Britain and had distinguished itself in the Dacian Wars under Trajan.

To obtain such a diploma was the ambition of every auxiliary—horse and foot alike—for it meant that the citizenship of Rome, probably the main inducement to enlist, was now theirs, and they were free to return home. Honourable discharge was normally achieved by serving out the agreed time period, some 25 years; and now that the auxiliary soldier was a citizen he would enjoy privileges under Roman law which also improved his family's prospects within the Roman system.

It appears that the Romans even took care over the morale of their auxiliaries, at least in the early days of the Empire, by posting the units fairly close to their place of origin, presumably in order to prevent feelings of disquiet among the troops at being cut off from familiar surroundings. Later, as necessity dictated, such niceties were overlooked and units were posted far afield, which occasioned at least two mutinies.

Naturally enough, the legionaries regarded the non-citizens of the *auxilia* as inferiors; but it was the auxiliaries who really manned the frontiers of the Empire and policed the Provinces, and it was they who fought and won the final battle of the invasion of Britain. Their contribution to the establishment of the Roman World may perhaps have been rather badly underestimated in favour of the 'esprit de corps' of the legions.

At the time of Vespasian some of the existing auxiliary units were enlarged and new units of greater strength were raised. These consisted of ten-century infantry cohorts, 24-troop cavalry regiments, and a ten-century cohort with eight cavalry troops as a larger form of *Cohors Equitata*. These new units were called *Milliaria* or 'thousand strong', but in fact contained rather fewer men. The smaller auxiliary units were called *Quingenaria* or 'five hundred strong', again being slightly weaker in practice than the title suggests.

As generations came and went, the sons of time-expired auxiliaries, now of citizen status, joined the same locally-based units with which their fathers had served; the rigid distinction between the legions and the *auxilia* began to fade, though it did not

conform to standard Roman unit strengths. Under Augustus, auxiliary units were integrated into the Roman army on a permanent basis, with a fixed annual recruitment, and organised after the Roman manner in three types of unit (see diagram). The infantry cohorts were named after either their tribal or national origin. The cavalry, on the other hand, were often identified by the name of the commanding officer in the early days, those titles remaining part of the unit's identification even though the man concerned was long dead: e.g. *Ala Augusta Gallorum* Petriana *Milliaria Civium Romanorum*—after Titus Pomponius Petra, whose name was to be found a century later when his old unit was serving on Hadrian's Wall at Carlisle.

The third type of auxiliary unit, the *Cohors Equitata*, was regarded as inferior to the other two, and this was clearly reflected in their equipment. Evidently this inferior status did not detract from the valour of the soldiers in one case at least, for a

finally disappear until the reign of the Emperor Caracalla in AD 212.

Entry, Training and Campaign Routines

Enrolment under normal circumstances, that is to say in time of comparable peace, was a rather similar process to that in use in some armies today. The applicant was ordered to appear before a board of examining officers, men experienced in the selection of the most suitable fighting material. The ideal was a man six *pes* tall (about five feet ten inches), of good eyesight and a strong, well-proportioned physique, a man of generally good bearing. After passing the board the young man, usually about 18 years old, began a period called *probatio*, during which he underwent a more stringent medical examination. His character would also be closely scrutinised during this period, and he would no doubt be asked many questions;

lazy men, thieves and the extremely immoral were not welcome in the Roman army, and when serious lapses did occur, such as a man being caught asleep on sentry duty, they were dealt with very severely indeed, often with fatal results.

Once accepted for service, recruits swore an oath of allegiance to the Emperor, probably before the Eagle of his legion, and was then posted to a special training camp, several examples of which have been identified in Britain. There the raw men were taught to dig ditches, build ramparts and look after their equipment, part of which they had to purchase out of their pay—usually the items which they would have had to buy in civil life as a matter of course.

Inescapably, a large part of the training was devoted to 'square-bashing' and route-marching with full equipment; learning how to adjust correctly the great legionary shield on a baldric, and how to carry the kit-pole in the left hand. As in any age, the recruits were no doubt awkward at first, but found these skills second nature by the time basic training was over.

The Romans exercised great care over rigidity of formation, since this was believed to be the key to safety on the march and success in battle. The legionaries were taught two paces, a short clipped step called, by the Roman historian Vegetius, the

A section of the relief of Trajan's Column showing legionaries building defences and setting up a ballista, while auxiliaries engage a force of Dacians. (Trajan's Column, Rome)

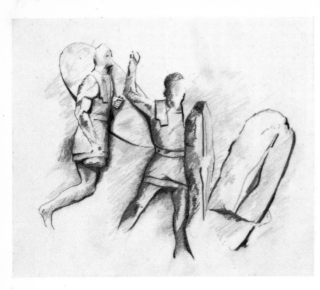

Mailed legionaries from the Aemilius Paulus victory monument at Delphi, erected to commemorate the Roman victory over King Perseus of Macedonia at Pydna in 168 BC. The shields are virtually identical to a surviving specimen from Egypt, which had a wooden boss covering the horizontal handgrip.

The thorax was avoided, most probably because that part of the torso has a superior natural defence and is not so easily pierced as the boneless abdomen. Cutting strokes were avoided as much as possible, though an enemy unhelmeted was clearly too tempting a target for a swift downward blow on the skull to be missed (as witness skeletal finds at Maiden Castle). However, such a stroke necessarily exposed the entire right side: better to keep the arm low and avoid the risk of a possible 'sucking wound' in the rib-cage, leading to lung collapse. The Romans were said to have despised enemies who laid about themselves with long slashing blades, and despatched them with ease.

The recruits would also be taught to use the legionary shield as a weapon as much as a defence. The boss of the shield was certainly used to punch opponents and the edge may also have been used to strike an enemy in the face; the latter method is shown in early gladiatorial sculpture, but might have required rather more strength to achieve than was possessed by the average soldier. Either method would doubtless have the effect of causing the enemy to raise his arms to steady himself, thereby exposing his abdomen to a quick stab from the Roman's sword to end the matter.

Whether or not the javelin had to be delivered with a high degree of accuracy is questionable: the Emperor Hadrian, reviewing troops, praised the accuracy of their throwing, but launching those dreadful weapons at a packed enemy force was bound to do fearful harm wherever these long iron heads struck. Caesar tells us that the javelin was capable of piercing the enemies' shields and pinning them together, proving to be so troublesome to

'military pace', doubtless employed when tight drill was required; and the 'full pace', a longer, easier gait, used on the march for long periods. Precisely how the Romans taught their men accurate marching steps is not known, but one guesses at something akin to a modern pace-stick. In any event, the Romans do not appear to have had drumbeats as an aid to the step, either in training or subsequently; in fact the drum seems to have been unknown in the Roman army.

On the march, the soldiers were expected to cover a distance of 20 Roman miles at the 'military pace' in five hours; when the 'full pace' was used, a distance of 24 miles was achieved in the same period of time. Taking the Roman mile as being 1,620 yards, the full pace is a rate of nearly four-and-a-half miles per hour: a good measure by most standards, this must surely have applied to troop movements on good roads, for it would have been quite impossible to have accomplished these distances over rough and probably hostile terrain.

No less important, of course, would be weapon training, particularly the correct use of the short sword. Recruits were encouraged to attack six-foot wooden stakes fixed into the ground, using dummy shields and swords. The Romans used their swords to stab, keeping the hilt low and thrusting at the face, abdominal cavity and legs of an opponent.

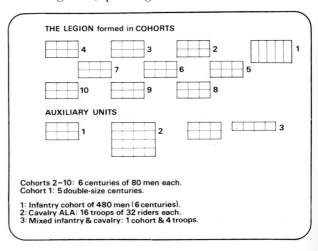

THE LEGION formed in COHORTS

Cohorts 2–10: 6 centuries of 80 men each.
Cohort 1: 5 double-size centuries.

1: Infantry cohort of 480 men (6 centuries).
2: Cavalry ALA: 16 troops of 32 riders each.
3: Mixed infantry & cavalry: 1 cohort & 4 troops.

A bronze boss from a *clipeus* or flat oval shield. Elaborately decorated with engraving and punching, it was most probably a cavalry piece used for the *hippika gymnasia* or cavalry sports.

The intricately decorated *scutum* boss which belonged to a legionary—Junius Dubitatus—who served with Legio VIII Augusta, presumably after AD 70 when that legion was stationed on the upper Rhine. Since the legion is not recorded as having been stationed in Britain, this find from the River Tyne on the north British frontier probably indicates the presence of a 'vexillation' or detachment only. (In the collection of the British Museum)

extricate that they preferred to drop the encumbered shields and face the legionaries unprotected. The extreme difficulty in removing the javelins probably describes the effect of a type of javelin head which had a small barbed tip, used in Caesar's time; an example was recovered from the site of the siege of Alesia, undertaken by Caesar during his conquest of Gaul.

The march and the marching camp

The legionaries illustrated as A3 and E2 in the colour plates show equipment slung for the march in friendly territory; this may be assumed from the position of the helmets, which would be worn on the march when hostilities were at all likely. Legionaries portrayed on Trajan's Column are shown to carry a pole in the left hand, apparently to support the soldiers' personal effects and mess equipment. This consisted of a bag which probably contained a military cloak or *sagum*, which may have doubled as a blanket; bathing and shaving tackle; spare thongs; equipment for scouring and polishing his armour and weapons; and doubtless his most prized possessions such as his decorations—such objects would not have been entrusted to the baggage train. Below the kit-bag may be seen the mess equipment: a mess tin or *patera*; a camp kettle; and a sack with a cord net protector, which probably held rations of

grain, bacon, cheese or any of the other extraordinary foods that may have been gathered by forage, said to have been eaten by Roman soldiers. A reinforced leather satchel is also shown on the Column, and this probably contained the soldier's tools for construction work. The remainder of the equipment belonging to each eight-man section (*contubernium*) was carried on a mule allotted to the section.

The order of march used by the legions as they advanced into Galilee during the Jewish uprising of AD 66–73 is given by the Jewish historian Joseph ben Matthias, better known as Flavius Josephus, in his extremely vivid and apparently accurate account of the insurrection—*The Jewish War*. Josephus refers to it as the 'usual' Roman marching order; however, one might expect a great deal to have depended upon the prevailing situation and the discretion of the army commander.

The vanguard was formed of light-armed auxiliaries and bowmen. These were to engage and

```
Orders of Seniority and Promotion


LEGATUS LEGIONIS
        |
   VIA SENATORIAL
   MAGISTRACIES
Tribunus Laticlavius                    Praefectus Alae M
                                              |
Primus Pilus Iterum                     Praefectus Alae D
Praefectus Castrorum                          |
                                        Tribunus Cohortis M
Tribuni Angusticlavii                         |
                                        Praefectus Cohortis D
   Primus Pilus      PRIMI
        |            ORDINES             INFANTRY        CAVALRY
Centuriones  coh. I
        |                               Centuriones     Decuriones
Centuriones coh. II–X                        |              |
        |                               Principales     Principales
   Principales                               |              |
        |                               Immunes         Immunes
   Immunes                                   |              |
        |                               Milites         Equites
   Milites

      LEGIONS                                 AUXILIA
```

repel skirmishers and to probe likely ambush cover. The head of the column proper was a body of heavily armed Roman troops, mounted and on foot. Next were the surveyors, drawn from the centuries of the legions, carrying the instruments for marking out a camp. Behind them came the pioneers (*antecursores*), probably carrying *dolabrae* for tree-felling and other tools. These men cleared the path of the army so that the already burdened soldiers would not be troubled further by difficult terrain. A strong cavalry force followed with the commander's baggage and that of his staff, behind which rode the commander himself, surrounded by the finest of his infantry and cavalry and a body of pikemen (*hastati*). Then came the legionary cavalry; Josephus indicates that there were 120 of these permanently attached to a legion, probably employed as scouts and messengers. These horsemen were followed by the 'artillery', consisting of *catapultae*, *ballistae*, rams and other war machinery carried in parts on mules. Behind these came the generals, cohort commanders and tribunes with their infantry guard marching before the sacred *aquila*, which was surrounded by the other legion standards and followed by the trumpeters with their instruments. The main column of infantry stretched out behind, marching six abreast in close dressing, with centurions watching the discipline of the formation. Next came the baggage-train with the tents and general construction implements, supervised by the camp 'servants'. The rear of the column was comprised of mercenaries, with a strong rearguard of infantry and cavalry whom one might believe were placed there as much to prevent the

mercenaries making off in the event of a serious assault being made against them, as to perform the normal duties of that office.

When the required distance had been covered, the surveyors (and presumably the pioneers) were sent forward to mark out a chosen site for the night camp. More conscientious commanders preferred to select the site in person. The size and construction of these 'marching camps' was laid down in manuals and they were like a playing-card in plan. From the remains of such camps it is evident that the plan was varied to suit the terrain, but mainly they adhere to the rectangular shape with rounded corners. The size of the camp was determined by a formula: 200 times the square root of the number of cohorts to be accommodated giving the short sides, one and one-half times that for the long sides.

The surveyors put up four big flags where the corners of the camp were to be and then marked off the positions of the four gates, one in each side. The two in the short sides were named *porta praetoria* and *porta decumana*. Those in the remaining sides were *porta principalis sinistra* and *porta principalis dextra*—left and right respectively from the main gate, the *porta praetoria*. The street plan of the camp was basically a cross, the *via praetoria* running between the main and rear gates and the *via principalis* between the side gates.

Assuming the site had been cleared and prepared by the pioneers and surveyors, the main body of the army now marched straight into the place without a halt, and dumped off kit in the areas allotted to each section; every man knew his own position, so all was accomplished without noise or delay. Men were detailed to throw up the enclosing rampart, which was usually quite shallow, little more than a yard wide and deep in the ditch, with the spoil thrown back to the camp side to form the rampart. *Pila muralia* or rampart stakes were then forced into the top of the bank and lashed together to form a palisade. These wooden stakes were about five feet in length, pointed at both ends and slightened in the middle to take the lashing.

While engaged in building such ramparts, the legionaries stacked their arms close at hand. The stack was made by ramming the shoe of the javelin into the ground and leaning the shield against it; the helmet was then tied to the shaft of the javelin and allowed to fall over the face of the shield, thus preventing the latter from being blown over. This method of stacking may be seen in several instances on Trajan's Column. The soldiers were required to wear their sidearms during construction of this nature, probably when the enemy was in the vicinity; one man is known to have been executed for not doing so, but this was probably an object lesson, since the event occurred during a known period of restoration of discipline.

Other men were posted as sentries, while the remainder set about erecting the sturdy leather tents in orderly lines with avenues between them. Their appearance was not unlike some modern ridge tents, with low verticals at the sides, and end-flaps. The main part of the tent was made from squares of goat hide, and sculptural representations of this feature gave rise to the misconception that Roman tents were provided with a rope net of large mesh. The tent covered an area of ten Roman feet square; the Roman foot or *pes* is equivalent to 0.962 foot Imperial measure.

Excavations of the Roman siege camps at the Herodian fortress of Masada have revealed that the tents were placed over recesses with side 'benches' dug into the ground, providing more standing room inside the tents; but it seems unlikely that tents would be 'dug in' like this for a night's marching camp, and this feature was probably more typical of camps which were to be inhabited for a considerable length of time.

Arms and Armour

Body Defences
In view of the understandable limitations of theatrical and film costume departments, they are obliged for one reason or another to persist in arming their Roman soldiers with defences constructed from leather; and since this image appears to impress itself upon unwitting audiences, it might not be unwise to include in this work a few words concerning the origin of the leather 'armour' so often used, and its lack of defensive quality.

This misconception arose very largely from the apparently common Roman habit of painting on to their sculptures parts which were tedious to portray with a chisel. They may also have reproduced the appearance of mail by making indentations into soft gesso with a curved tool. By the time the artists of the Renaissance began to portray the classical warrior, most or all of the painted or plastered parts had weathered away, leaving the mail shirts looking smooth and very like leather jerkins. Perhaps if the artists had taken the trouble to look closely at the representations of auxiliaries on Trajan's Column, they would have observed that the 'jerkins' were in fact worked with close-set vertical zigzag lines, clearly intended to represent the texture of mail.

If one examines leather as a defensive material and then tries to reconcile its properties with the forms of body defence used by the Romans, it becomes perfectly apparent that it would have been quite useless: either it would not have been proof against the weapons of the ancient world, or if it *had* been thick and hard enough to withstand a spear thrust or sword cut, the wearer would have experienced extreme difficulty in performing any normal movements, let alone the violent motions required in an action.

Plan of the common *caliga* **laid out flat. These boots were provided with soles approximately ½ in thick and heavily studded with domed hobnails of iron.**

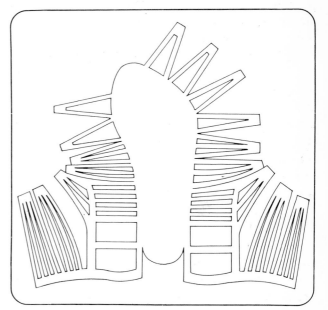

Leather did feature to some extent in this period, but only as *pteruges*, the series of hide strips appended to corselets of mail, scale or plate armour. No doubt the hide used for *pteruges* would have been somewhat akin to the 'buff leather' so familiar in portrayals of soldiers of the 17th century—though since the latter type requires an extract from the sperm whale for its manufacture, the similarity would be slight. It is interesting, however, to note how little faith was actually placed in the buff coats, as evidenced by the addition of an iron cuirass and a bridle or elbow gauntlet on the left forearm.

To return to the Romans, the addition of *pteruges*

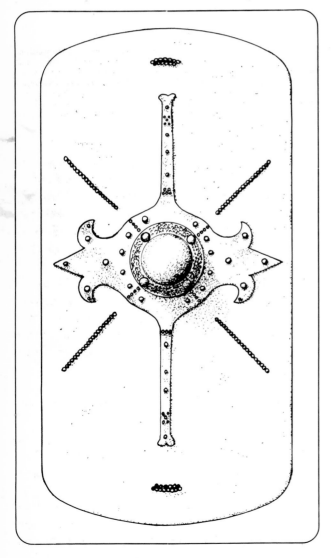

The auxiliary shield from Doncaster, thought to have belonged to the garrison of Danum in the second half of the 1st century AD. An example of auxiliary troops continuing to carry native equipment. Rectangular shields were uncommon among auxiliaries, but may be seen occasionally in sculpture.

would have meant a valuable saving in mail manufacture, and it seems that to that end they were prepared to sacrifice some of the highly effective protection afforded to the upper arm and thigh.

Precisely which nation was responsible for the invention of mail, called *hamata* by the Romans, remains a matter for debate. The earliest examples of mail are quoted as having been found in Scythian tombs of the 5th century BC; however, it seems most unlikely that people such as the Scythians, who enjoyed a nomadic way of life, would have been able to develop the quite advanced tooling required for successful mail manufacture. The next indication of the use of mail is a painting of a mercenary soldier from Galatia (modern Turkey, but an area apparently settled in early times by Celtic peoples) wearing a short, sleeveless hauberk, dated to the 3rd or 2nd century BC. The Roman writer Varro states that the Romans acquired their knowledge of mail-making from the Celtic Gauls, and it was considered that they were its inventors. Whilst there is no evidence to prove or disprove Varro on this point, the Celts were an inventive people with a superb mastery of metal working, perfectly able to achieve such an innovation. But exactly the same can equally well be said of the peoples of the Middle East—the Assyrians made beautiful iron helmets as early as the 8th to 7th centuries BC (see British Museum) and therefore the required technology could very possibly have been developed in that region.

Whether mail originated in western Europe or in the Middle East, in view of the Scythian finds its date of origin must surely be as early as the 6th century BC; and its continued use by the Romans is evidenced initially by the Aemilius Paulus victory monument at Delphi, dated to the first half of the 2nd century BC, and the altar of Domitius Ahenobarbus, dated to the second half of the 1st century BC. Both these sculptures depict legionaries wearing mail defences, the essential difference between them being that those of the latter appear to have been slightly lengthened in the main body of the hauberks.

The Romans appear to have inherited two types of shoulder doublings: one was cut in a fashion reminiscent of Greek linen cuirasses, and the second in a form of cape, more probably of Celtic origin, which did not require leathering in its early form (though the Romans appear to have used leathers to back both types by the 1st century AD). This was clearly necessary in the case of the Greek type, which collapses into long, narrow strips when unleathered, and is totally unworkable.

As a defence, mail has two very considerable drawbacks: it is extremely laborious to make, and while it affords complete freedom of movement to the wearer, it is very heavy. The manufacturing difficulty was partly overcome by the use of alternate rows of stamped rings which did not require to be joined. These must have been a blessing to the ancient mail-maker, and it would be most interesting to know what kind of tools they used to make them. The stamped rings still had to be linked together with riveted wire rings, but the time involved in making a complete hauberk must have been cut by as much as a quarter. A less costly form of mail, probably Celtic, employed stamped rings in the same manner, but the wire rings were simply cut from the coil and left as a butted circlet, without riveting.

The weight of the mail, when unbelted, fell entirely onto the wearer's shoulders, and with a hauberk which weighed perhaps as much as 15lbs this would be very tiring and more than a little uncomfortable. This was countered by the military belt drawn tightly about the waist, thereby causing part of the weight to be distributed onto the hips; the use of *pteruges* could also reduce the drag of the mail.

The use by the Romans of scale shirts (*loricae squamatae*), judging by their sculptures, does not appear to have been as extensive as mail, with the possible exception of the cavalry, and the infantry officer class, including the *principales*. This is hardly surprising, since as a defence, scale was far inferior to mail, being neither as strong nor as flexible. The scales were never thick enough to withstand a good cut and remain undamaged; and the hauberk could be pierced with relative ease by an upthrust of sword or spear, which would have made it rather an unsatisfactory defence for a cavalry trooper engaging footsoldiers armed with spears.

The method of manufacture was to overlap the scales and fasten them together in horizontal rows by means of loose, rough rings passed through small holes in the sides of the scales. The rows were then

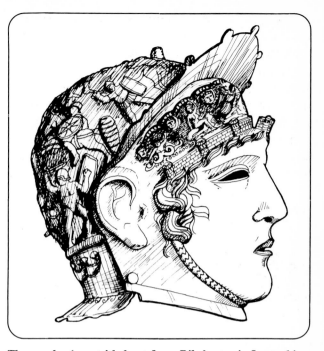

The cavalry 'sports' helmet from Ribchester in Lancashire. The mask was hinged at the top and tied down with a strap and buckle round the nape. The helmet is of bronze and had a silvered face. It was fitted with a crest, most probably of horse-hair, and streamers, perhaps of the same material, tied to rings at the sides of the skull. This very fine example of the armourer's art may be seen in the British Museum.

applied to the foundation of rough linen (or occasionally, thin hide) by laying a strand of yarn along the face of the scales over the larger holes in the upper edges and then stitching through the holes and round the yarn. This had the effect of minimising the metal's tendency to fray the stitching-thread.

Scale did have its advantages: it could be made by virtually anyone, and was very simple to repair. Cost, just as much of a problem to the ancients as it is today, was doubtless a consideration—scale armour of the more common types was cheap in comparison with mail.

It was probably early in the reign of the Emperor Tiberius that the first type of laminated iron cuirass (*lorica segmentata*) made its appearance, perhaps as a result of the enormous loss of equipment that was suffered by the Rhine legions in AD 9. The replacement of all the lost material must have presented a considerable problem, for mail shirts are very time consuming in manufacture. The iron plate *segmentata*, by contrast, could be made with the equipment available to the Romans in probably no more than 60 hours, given the sheet iron.

These remarkably flexible armours were probably the first iron plate defences ever devised, and may have been partially developed from gladiatorial equipment. Whether or not they were a purely Roman invention is not certain; however, there is no evidence to suggest otherwise. The idea of using lames in the construction of simple armguards was known to the Greeks, but it is a very

The pierced, engraved and silvered locket of a 'Pompeii' pattern sword scabbard. The two figures are representations of the war-god Mars. The piece probably had palmettes at the lower corners.

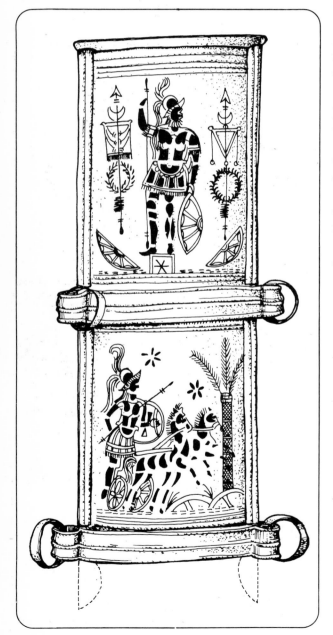

considerable step to the production of entire cuirasses.

It is certain that the cuirass now classified as Corbridge 'A' was quite widely issued by the time the Emperor Claudius ordered the invasion of Britain in AD 43, and the recent discovery of an unused shoulder-splint plate conforming very closely to the type 'B' cuirass, found on the site of the invasion supply base of Legio II Augusta at Chichester, suggests that the second of the Corbridge cuirass types was already in circulation by that date.

While hundreds of fragments from cuirasses of this type have been found on sites where legionaries have been present, and reconstructions attempted, it is only as a result of excavations in 1964 on the site of the Roman station of Corstopitum (Corbridge) near Hadrian's Wall that the true appearance and construction of these armours has become established. Buried beneath the floor of one of the Roman buildings, the remains of an iron-bound chest was discovered, containing, among other items, bundles of completely oxidised iron armour. From these have emerged the two patterns of cuirass of 1st century date known as Corbridge 'A' and 'B'; the major difference between them is the method used to fasten the girdle unit to the collar sections (see colour plates E2 and E3).

The laminated cuirasses were obviously superior to mail with regard to ease of manufacture and preservation, but most particularly in view of their weight, which was as little as 12lbs, depending upon the thickness of plate used. Inevitably, they had some disadvantages as well, notably the loss of protection to the thighs and upper arms. Quality control in manufacture also provided something of a problem; weak or badly made fittings, which frequently broke, must have given the legionary armourers a continual round of repairs, and it was not until the later years of the 1st century that a new type of cuirass was developed which was devoid of almost all fittings which would break easily and were not really necessary. This type of cuirass, which we call the 'Newstead' (see colour plate F3), after fragments found on the site of the fort of Trimontium (Newstead) near Melrose, Scotland, was strong and perfectly functional. It is this pattern which is to be seen in the majority of the representations on Trajan's Column.

What is most probably a fourth type of cuirass, similar to the Newstead, is shown in various sculptures and small figurines. This pattern, actual remains of which have yet to be discovered, is clearly depicted on a section of the frieze from Trajan's Forum (see photographic plate), which was subsequently re-used in the construction of the Arch of Constantine. Instead of the single-piece breast-plates of the Newstead pattern, this type apparently was fitted with continuous laminations all the way up to the neck, in much the same way as the upper back-plates of the Corbridge cuirasses had been.

Helmets

The head-pieces worn by Caesar's legionaries were more often of the rather simple and not very well finished Montefortino type 'C' shown in colour plate A1. Such helmets were clearly mass-produced, probably as a result of the Marian reforms which had permitted enlistment in the legions by large numbers of poor men, who could not afford to purchase costly armour, as had been the custom previously. These helmets were crested with a brush and tail of horse-hair mounted on a single pin, which was inserted into a drill-hole in the knob on the top of the helmet crown. Helmets of this type continued in service during the 1st century AD.

During the reign of the Emperor Augustus the first of the 'Coolus' helmets appeared in the Roman army. These had a more natural skull shape to the bowl and a larger neck-guard than the Montefortino pattern. The skull form was of Gallic origin, the earliest specimen having been found in the Marne

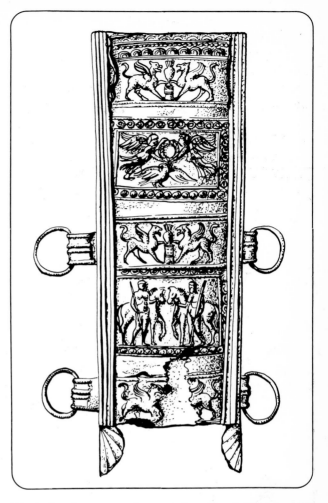

The locket from a cavalry sword scabbard. The stamped decoration on the face is applied thin bronze sheet, and the style of decoration suggests a cavalry unit of Thracian origin.

Basin. The Roman version was somewhat improved by the addition of a frontal reinforce or 'peak' which prevented blows from striking the forepart of the skull. The early Roman Coolus helmets of type 'C' had no crest fastenings, unlike almost all of their

A leather tent—*papilio*—reconstructed from goat hide fragments found at Newstead in Scotland by the late Sir Ian Richmond. The tent housed an eight-man section called a *contubernium*.

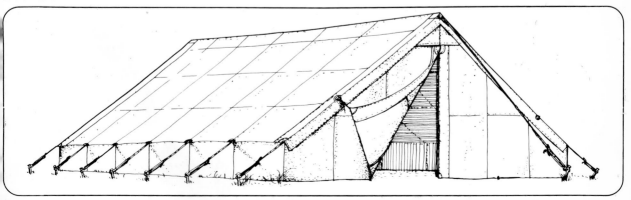

cousins. Coolus type 'E', shown in figure A3, is based on the well-known Walbrook helmet, which may be seen in the British Museum; this helmet not only had a spike for the attachment of a central horse-hair crest, but thin bronze tubes soldered to the sides of the skull for the mounting of plumes (see

author's reconstruction of a Coolus 'E' helmet). Cresting practices may have varied from legion to legion, according to its area of origin, or its status, or possibly there may be some significance of rank for which the evidence is currently obscure.

The first half of the 1st century AD saw a very much larger neck-guard develop, culminating in the Haguenau helmet—Coolus type 'G'—in the third quarter of the century. The Haguenau specimen has a flat, almost semi-circular neck-

Four views of an Imperial Italic type 'C' bronze helmet from the River Po, probably lost during the civil war of AD 68–69, which began with the suicide of Nero and ended with the establishment of the Flavian dynasty. (In the collection of the Museo Stibbert, Florence)

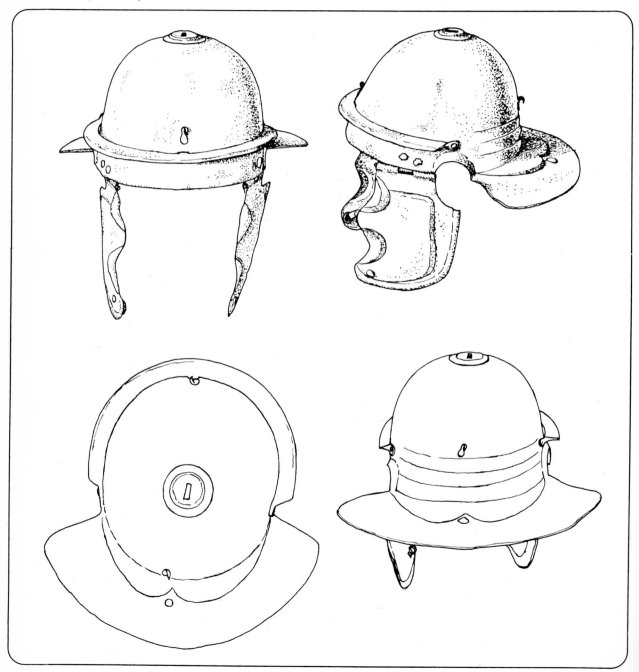

guard and a bulbous skull of considerable height, with a crest spike and side-tubes for plumes. At about the same time a new pattern of bronze helmet was being made, probably in Italy, of which two specimens survive (see author's drawings of the Imperial Italic type 'C' helmet from the River Po at Cremona). Both of these helmets contain Gallic features which are common to the iron helmets of this date, but have no eyebrows and are fitted with crest fastenings of Italian type (see colour plate C1).

The production of iron helmets had been practiced in Gaul prior to the subjugation by Caesar in the mid-1st century BC, and once the Gauls were incorporated into the Roman sphere the iron helmet began to appear in the ranks of the legions. Colour plate E shows three types of iron helmet that had been evolved by the middle years of the 1st century AD, denoted Imperial Gallic types 'F' and 'E'. The helmets of Gallic origin were usually of a superior finish to those produced by the factories of Italy at that time—probably because iron working is very much more difficult than bronze, and the technology was new to the Italian armourers.

The iron helmets were frequently decorated with small stamped bosses, sometimes with fine ribbing and red enamelled centres—a typically Celtic feature. The peaks were occasionally provided with a fine strip of reeded bronze along the forward edge, but one is inclined to feel that such intricacies would not have survived for more than a matter of minutes in action. Oddly enough, none of the surviving helmets bear marks which can be attributed with any certainty to combat damage. The helmet of Italic type 'D' from the River Rhine at Mainz displays a series of nicks along the forward edge of the peak which were thought to be the results of an action; however, the marks in question are placed at very regular intervals, which can only mean that they were introduced deliberately, most probably in modern times.

The manufacture of iron helmets did not preclude the continued supply of bronze head-pieces, as may be seen by the author's reconstruction of the Mainz bronze legionary helmet, also illustrated in colour plate F1, which was made during the mid-second half of the 1st century AD. No doubt the continued manufacture of bronze pieces was partly caused by the very slow trickle of iron

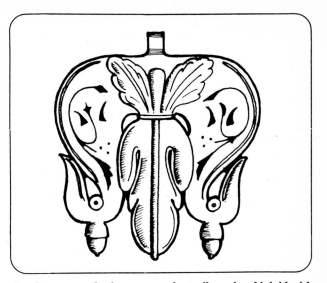

Cast bronze cavalry harness pendant, silvered and inlaid with black niello. These pendants were normally suspended below a *phalera* or decorated disc by means of the pierced lug at the top. (After Dr. Graham Webster)

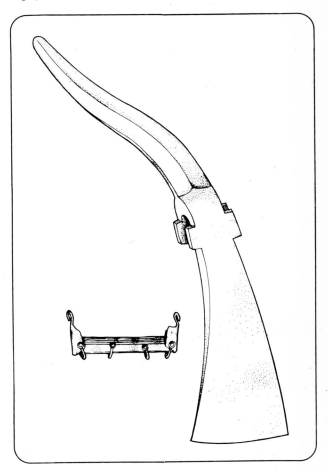

The *dolabra*—military pickaxe. These were provided with angled metal guards to cover the axe edge, tied on by means of thongs.

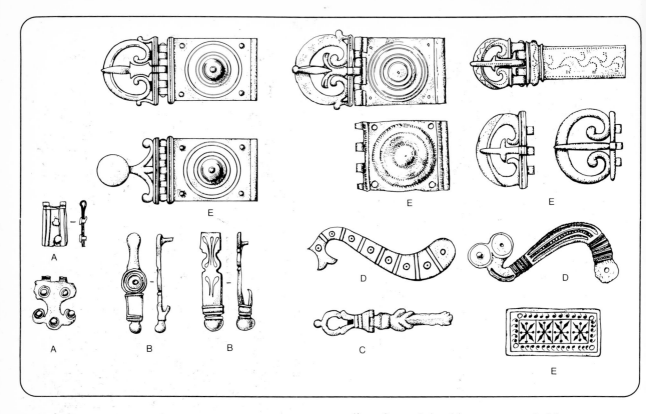

(a) Fittings from a *lorica segmentata*, with crude decoration. (b) Cavalry harness decorations. (c) Baldric fastener with a hinged loop. (d) Types of breasthooks from mail shirts. (e) Belt fittings, usually tinned or silvered.

helmets from the arms factories—a large *fabricia* could only supply six per month.

The first true cavalry helmets probably emerged during the first half of the 1st century AD and consisted of an iron skull with a deep back and iron cheek-guards, the whole being skinned over with thin embossed bronze sheet (see colour plates H1 and H2). The only specimen of one of these skinned helmets to have survived in a reasonably good state of preservation was found at Witcham Gravel in Cambridgeshire and is now in the British Museum. The steep angle and size of the neck-guard suggest that the piece was made during the third quarter of the 1st century AD.

The helmets of the auxiliary infantry, as may be seen in colour plate D2, were very much simpler than their legionary counterparts and were sometimes made by a process known today as 'metal-spinning'. The example illustrated is based on the skull found at Flüren in Germany. This method of manufacture is accomplished by forcing a disc of metal, in this case annealed bronze, over a former of either wood or metal revolving in a type of lathe. An interesting point arises in connection with this method of manufacture. We know today that a considerable amount of power is required to operate a spinning lathe and one may well wonder how the Romans managed to generate such a force. It is also known that medieval armoury workshops employed power supplied by water-wheels to turn their machinery such as large grindstones, and this practice was continued for the manufacture of agricultural implements as late as the early Industrial Revolution. Could it possibly be the case that the Romans, to whom this form of power was known, also employed it for such purposes?

The sword

The *gladius* of Caesarian to Tiberian date, with its fine broad-shouldered and long-pointed blade, while being somewhat heavy, was probably one of the most aesthetically pleasing objects the Romans ever produced, and was a descendant of the weapon of the Spanish Celts.

The hilt was made in three parts: the guard, with a recessed underside lined with a bronze plate; the grip, usually of bone; and the pommel, surmounted

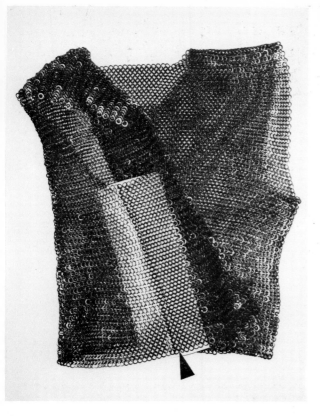

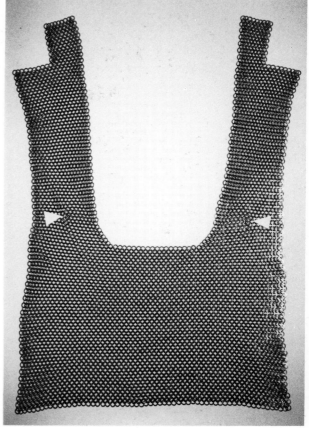

(Left) Piece of a mail hauberk of unriveted link made by the author, showing the probable position of the join discovered in the Carlingwark Loch fragment (arrowed). (Right) An entire unleathered shoulder doubling of Greek type, laid out to show expansions (arrowed) necessary to achieve a good fit. This piece of mail would have been joined to the main body of the hauberk with a single line of rings across the base of the back.

by a bronze terminal which held the parts in position on the blade's tang. The grips were usually of octagonal section, occasionally hexagonal, with four concave finger-grips carved into each of the surfaces, producing a very desirable effect which gave the soldier an excellent hold on the weapon. The guards and pommels were sometimes made from hardwood, doubtless producing a cheaper weapon than those that used ivory for these parts. A more expensive version of the hilt was found together with its blade at Rheingonheim: this was made from wood, but encased with silver plate.

The scabbard for this pattern of sword was, as is usual with scabbards, basically wooden with a leather covering sewn on while wet. This sheathing, together with a full-length face-plate, was slipped into a metal frame of side-gutters and cross-bands soldered into a terminal at the lower end; once the sheathing was in position, the scabbard was capped

with a locket which was secured with a pin driven through the back of the locket and the wooden liner, being bent over on the inside of the scabbard.

The face-plate sometimes bore decoration in the form of embossed slips which showed either side of the cross-bands and had elaborately pierced or embossed locket and chape plates. Some swords bore a roundel displaying the Emperor's image encircled with a wreath ('Sword of Tiberius', British Museum).

A slightly later pattern is represented by swords of the Fulham type (see author's reconstruction), named after the specimen recovered from the River Thames and now in the British Museum. The face-plate shown in the model does not belong to the original Fulham Sword, the scabbard of which was incomplete. These were the first swords known to have employed the parallel edges of the blade so characteristic of the later Romans. The broad shoulders remain, though the overall width has been lessened. The long point is also in evidence, but the slight and graceful curve of the Celtic ancestors has entirely disappeared. The hilt is

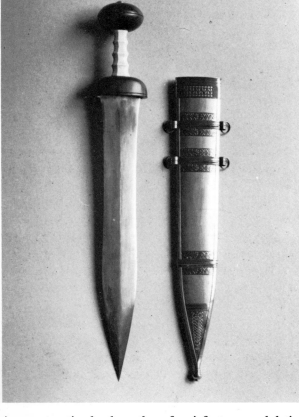

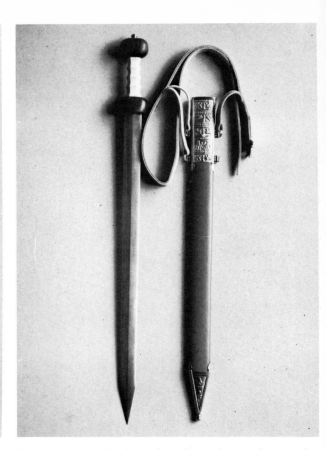

A reconstruction by the author of an infantry sword dating from the reign of Augustus Caesar, modelled on the remains of a scabbard from Mainz, with pierced decoration, and a blade of similar pattern to the badly corroded original found on the Chapel Street site, Chichester. The original blade may be seen in the Chichester District Museum.

A reconstruction by the author of a *spatha*—cavalry sword—dating from the 1st century AD, modelled on a blade found at Newstead near Melrose, Scotland, now in the National Museum of Antiquities of Scotland, and a locket of unknown provenance belonging to a weapon of this type. The belt and chape are hypothetical.

hypothetical.

During the first half of the 1st century AD and certainly before the invasion of Britain, a new pattern of *gladius* had emerged; this was to set the final shape of Roman infantry swords until barbarian influence superseded the arms and armour of Celtic origin. These swords, which we call the Pompeii pattern after the three specimens found amongst the ruins of that city (see author's reconstruction of a Pompeii-pattern sword, also the Long Windsor type), had short, strong points and completely parallel edges.

There was also a completely new form of scabbard introduced at this time, apparently for both the infantry and cavalry swords. This consisted of the normal sheath, but the side-gutters and face-plate had been made obsolete, being replaced by the separate lockets and chapes shown in the author's reconstructions. This type of

scabbard may have been the final truly Roman pattern, and despite the depiction of scabbards with side-gutters in sculpture, the older pattern was probably never reverted to.

Short swords were normally worn on the right side, and, in view of their relatively short blades, were drawn by inverting the hand to grasp the hilt and pushing the pommel forward. The scabbards obviously had to be very free to permit this method of draw; a weapon which jammed in its scabbard would have been disastrous to its owner.

The shield

The great curved legionary shield—*scutum*—is thought to have been Celtic in origin, being derived from flat oval shields made from a single layer of timber for the main shield board. The introduction of a lateral curvature would have meant the introduction of the early form of plywood described by the historian Polybius, who wrote a reasonably explicit description of the Roman army during the 2nd century BC. The early type was made from two layers of wood glued together and then covered with canvas and hide, the upper and lower edges being bound with iron. The shields of Caesar's time were probably much like that discovered at Kasr el Harit in Egypt, known as the 'Fayum Scutum'. This specimen, the only early example of a *scutum* yet discovered, was made from three layers of wooden strips and was covered with woolen felt; presumably the latter was a substitute for the canvas covering and the Fayum shield may have been formerly covered with hide, which was subsequently removed. Like most oval shields of the period, this specimen has ribs or 'spines' on the face, a feature which the Romans continued to employ up to the end of the 1st century BC.

It was probably during the second half of that century that the *scutum* underwent its first stage of alteration towards the semi-cylindrical form; the upper and lower curves were removed (see author's reconstruction), and at about the turn of the century or a little later, the shield board seems to have been made lighter; this necessitated the introduction of back-bracing, evidenced by the presence of 'L' shapes in the corners on the face of these shields (Arch of Orange and grave stele of C. Valerius Crispus).

By the middle of the 1st century AD the final semi-cylindrical *scutum* had appeared, and this seems to have remained the basic shape of the legionary shield until it was replaced in the late Empire by large circular types. An example of what is probably a late *scutum* was found at Dura-Europos on the River Euphrates. It was considered to be a piece of parade equipment for many years; however, there is nothing to support this assertion, and the Dura *scutum* represents the furthest development of the Celtic shield in the mid-3rd century, shortly before it became obsolete.

The javelin
There were, generally speaking, two types of pole weapon in the Roman army: the *hasta* or thrusting spear with a leaf-shaped blade, and the *pilum* or javelin.

Because the remains of two different patterns of javelin were found on the site of the siege of Alesia, it is considered that the legionaries of Caesar's time were still carrying two *pila* each, as they had done in the previous century—one heavy type with a large splice-block to increase its weight, and a lighter socketed type for use at longer range. However, the description of the opening of the engagement between Caesar's legions and those of Pompey the Great at Pharsalus seems to indicate the carriage of only one *pilum* per man, and it is possible that the practice had changed by that date.

By the middle of the 1st century AD the splice-type *pilum* had become lighter, judging by three specimens found in the fort at Oberaden in Germany; and a new pattern of much heavier type had also been introduced. The latter had a tapered shaft fitted with a heavy lead load just behind the slightly shorter splice-block, which held a shorter iron head than the earlier patterns. The purpose of the load was obviously to increase the penetrative ability of the weapon, and when handling this javelin it becomes clear that it was intended to be used at fairly close range. The Cancelleria Relief at Rome shows men of the Praetorian Guard parading with similar weapons which have eagle motifs cast on the loads; it is most unlikely that this would have been a feature of the common field javelin, and it is practicably possible that the Praetorians' *pila* were provided with bronze loads instead of the usual lead ones. Such an image cast on a lead object would not

The common Roman military boot used by both infantry and cavalry, shown here with a spur found at Hod Hill, Dorset. Reconstruction by the author.

have survived for very long in normal daily life; a single light blow against a wall would destroy at least part of the emblem.

It is difficult to tell whether or not each legionary carried more than one javelin at this date, for there were many different variations on the same theme; sculpture, for what it may be worth as evidence, does not show legionaries carrying more than one each, while auxiliaries are shown to carry as many as three pole weapons at once (Mainz Praetorium).

The military belt and dagger

The belt, or *cingulum militare*, as previously mentioned, began its life as a means of distributing the weight of mail onto the wearer's hips and for the carriage of the sword and dagger. During the reign of Augustus the practice was to wear two belts, one for each sidearm.

In the early 1st century AD the groin-guard, or 'sporran' as it has been called, made its appearance. Initially it was copied from the Celtic practice of cutting the tie-end of a belt into four strips, using

Author's reconstruction of the Imperial Gallic type 'I' helmet from the River Rhine at Mainz. Only the skull of the original helmet survived; the cheek-guards are restored, based on a contemporary pattern. (Part of a complete equipment made by the author for the Rijksmuseum G.M. Kam, Nijmegen, Netherlands)

only one of these to fasten the belt, all four being fitted with small terminals. By the middle of the century the groin-guard had become a separate item attached to one of the belts—usually that for the dagger—and some were very elaborate affairs. The fittings of the 1st century were of enormous variety, usually being tinned or silvered; in some cases the embossed relief stamped into the thin bronze with cast dies was left unsilvered, to provide a beautiful effect against the ground. Others were inlaid with black niello, as were many cavalry harness fittings. The military belt began to go out of favour towards the end of the 1st century; there is evidence of a reduction of the groin-guard in the case of legionaries, and its total cessation of issue to the auxilia.

The dagger (*pugio*) was, like the *gladius*, of Spanish origin, and was sometimes a very well-made piece of equipment with highly ornate decoration of silver or gold with red enamel inlay on the scabbard and sometimes the hilt as well (Colchester Museum). The most common form of construction was a blade and hilt silhouette with horn applied to both sides of the hilt, probably worked to the form shown in the author's reconstruction; a skinning of either thin bronze or iron was then applied to the outside and riveted

1: Legionary infantryman, late Republic period
2, 3: Legionary infantrymen, late Augustan to Tiberian period

A

1: Centurio, Legio II Augusta, late Augustan to Tiberian period
2: Signifer, Legio XIV Gemina, Tiberian period
3: Aquilifer, Legio XI Claudia Pia Fidelis, mid-1st C. AD

B

1: Legionary infantryman, Legio VIII Augusta, mid-1st C. AD
2: Aquilifer, Legio XIV Gemina, first half 1st C. AD
3: Centurio, Legio XI Claudia Pia Fidelis, mid-1st C. AD

C

1: Signifer, Cohors V Asturum, 1st C. AD
2: Auxiliary infantryman, mid-1st C. AD
3: Imagnifer, 1st C. AD

D

1: Centurio, Legio XX Valeria, mid-1st C. AD
2: Legionary infantryman, mid-1st C. AD
3: Legionary infantryman, second half 1st C. AD

E

1: Legionary infantryman, Legio II Adiutrix, late 1st C. AD
2: Auxiliary infantryman of a Cohors Equitata, Trajanic period
3: Legionary infantryman, Trajanic period

F

1: Provincial legate, early Imperial period
2: Junior tribune, early Imperial period
3: Cornicen, Trajanic period

G

1: Cavalry trooper, Ala Noricum, second half 1st C. AD
2: Cavalry trooper, Ala Noricum, mid-1st C. AD

H

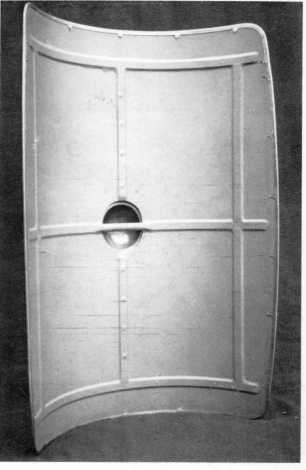

(Left) A curve-sided *scutum* (hypothetical reconstruction by the author) of Augustan date. The ribs on the face are a survival from much earlier shields of this type. (Right) The back of the same shield showing bracing, thought to have been introduced during the reign of Augustus to stiffen a lighter shield-board. Part of a complete equipment made by the author for the Riveredge Foundation, Calgary, Canada)

through. The use of either metal would have matched that employed for the scabbard. The scabbard construction was simple, but very effective. The main plate of the scabbard was worked back round the edges and soldered to a thin back-plate. The side-rings were attached by means of nails passed right through the sides of the scabbard and simply bent over on the rear. The dagger ceased to be issued at the end of the 1st century AD.

Conclusion

The limitations of space in a book of this size prevent any discussion here of the course of specific campaigns fought by the Roman army in our period. These may be found in many standard works of history; and since all are based on a relatively—and tragically—fragmentary surviving body of Roman historical writing, such as Tacitus' *Annals of Imperial Rome*, which is generally available in inexpensive translations, the author must leave it to the interested reader to pursue his research elsewhere. The remit for a Men-at-Arms author is, after all, to concentrate upon the physical detail of

25

Author's reconstruction of a 'Fulham' pattern sword and scabbard. These swords are named after an incomplete specimen recovered from the River Thames. The example shown has an embossed face-plate from Germany and the original Fulham blade-form, locket, frame and terminal. This pattern was probably developed in the Roman Rhineland during the early 1st century AD, with a fairly limited production, giving way to the 'Pompeii' type during the reign of Tiberius. (In the collection of Mr. T. W. Rath, Vermont, USA)

his subject, which in this case is certainly varied and fascinating enough to occupy many times the available space.

In conclusion, however, it is surely permissible to add that the debt owed today by European (and thus by extension, North American) culture and civilisation to the long-dead legionaries and auxiliaries of Rome is incalculable. Through their army the Romans not only conquered new lands, but brought the benefits of their civilisation to countries where internal warfare had been a way of life. Many of those benefits were secured through the hard work and skill of the legionaries, in their role as the only organised force of craftsmen and engineers available to the new provinces.

Though at times the Romans were responsible for some astounding cruelties, it should be remembered that most peoples of their time engaged in what we today would regard as unacceptable behaviour in civilised society. It would be an entirely distorted reading of history to believe that they were morally very different from the peoples they subjugated.

Generally speaking, the advantages to be gained from belonging to the Roman world were very great. The greatest force for happiness throughout human history, after all, has been the expectation of ordinary people that they can live their lives, tend their land and raise their children in peace. The Roman army created conditions in which, for centuries on end, a farmer could normally hope to till his fields secure in the knowledge that a marauding band from a neighbouring tribe would not be permitted to carry off the fruit of his labour, and probably to slaughter or enslave him and his family into the bargain.

Under the *Pax Romana* a man could travel from Palmyra in Syria to Eburacum in north Britain without a passport and without ever feeling entirely out of place. Wherever he went, Rome had established a miniature version of the mother city, with markets, baths, temples, and all the other complexities of the 'Roman way'. It was for the establishment of these benefits and the maintenance of that order that the Roman army was directly responsible; and though, for many different reasons, the outer fabric eventually fell into ruin, the all-important core of that experience remains with us today. So perhaps the noble Romans' wish and belief is a reality after all: ROMA AETERNA EST!

The Plates

A1: Legionary infantryman, late Republic period

The reconstruction is largely based on a figure shown in the reliefs on the Altar of Domitius Ahenobarbus in the Louvre. The sculpture portrays legionaries wearing long sleeveless mail hauberks with shoulder doubling, which in this case appears to have been leathered on the face of the mail, in order that decoration could be applied.

The helmet is of Montefortino type 'C', which may be regarded as plain state issue armour, with a horse-hair crest attached to the helmet by means of a single pin inserted vertically into the knob on the crown.

The shield is the early *scutum*, measuring approximately four feet in height. Shields of this type were most probably developed from Celtic flat oak patterns which were made from a single board, tapered towards the edges. Whilst the horizontal grip and wooden boss remained the same, the Roman introduction of a lateral curve necessitated the invention of a form of plywood for the shield board.

A2: Legionary infantryman, late Augustan to Tiberian period

The body defence of this figure is based on a representation on the Arch of Orange (Arausio), which was erected in the reign of Tiberius to commemorate the suppression by Legio II Augusta of a Gallic revolt in AD 21. The main defence is again mail, but with protection to the thighs being afforded by a kilt of *pteruges*, pendant strips of hide, which have also been added to the upper arms. The *pteruges* would have been attached to an arming doublet, probably of hide, worn beneath the mail corselet. The shoulder doubling is backed and piped with hide and braced across the chest with a double

Author's reconstruction of a *lorica segmentata* **of Corbridge type 'A', found on the site of the Roman supply base of Corstopitum near to Corbridge in Northumberland. (In the collection of the Lancashire Schools Museum Service)**

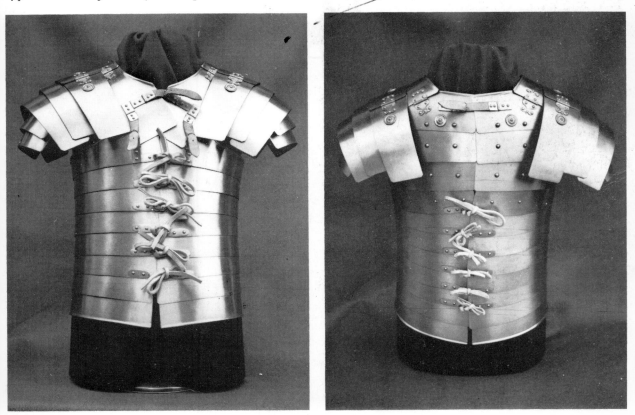

hook device; the latter prevented the doubling 'straps' from slipping outwards, their natural tendency.

The helmet is of Coolus type 'C', based on an example from Schaan, Liechtenstein. This type of head-piece was very well made, with relatively heavy frontal reinforces or 'peaks' to prevent blows from striking the helmet bowl. The fastening strap would have had slits near to the ends which were simply pressed over projecting studs on the outside of the cheek-guards. It is difficult to understand why the Romans did not make greater use of this very fast method of securing the helmet, instead of using thongs tying beneath the chin.

The shield shows the first stage of alteration towards the semi-cylindrical form of *scutum* of later periods. The top and bottom curves have been removed, reducing the height to about three feet four inches. The side curves remain, perhaps also the tapering thickness of the shield board. By this date waist belts were being worn in pairs, one for each sidearm.

A3: Legionary infantryman, late Augustan to Tiberian period

The long mail hauberk of this figure is also based on the reliefs of the Arch of Orange and appears to be the more common of the two types. The lengthening of the body of the hauberk has rendered the 'kilt' of *pteruges* unnecessary; however, they remain in the deltoid region, and it may be that the Romans had not learned to tailor their mail to make a satisfactory shoulder-cap by this date. The Gauls appear to have been able to overcome this slight problem in the manufacture of similar body defences. An excellent example is the fine statue of a late Celtic warrior from Vacheres, southern France. Presumably the upper arm *pteruges* would have still required an arming doublet.

The helmet, here shown slung for the march in friendly territory, is of Coolus type 'E' and is based on the Walbrook helmet in the British Museum. Unlike the Schaan helmets, this pattern was fitted with a solid bronze crest spike and side tubes for plumes. The central crest would have been a brush and tail of horse-hair similar to the late Republic type, but with a small crest-box to hold the hair in a more erect manner.

The shield is shown with its temporary goat hide cover for the march. Such covers were probably only removed for sentry duty or when an engagement was imminent. On the march, the shield was carried on a baldric, which allowed the soldier to carry his kit pole with his left hand. Experiment has shown that it is necessary to strap the shield up high in the manner shown here, in order to clear the man's legs in motion.

B1: Centurio, Legio II Augusta, late Augustan to Tiberian period

This figure also appears on the reliefs of the Arch of Orange and is easily identifiable as a centurion by his greaves. The body defence is very similar to that of figure A3, except that the centurion wears a medallion of the Gorgon Medusa suspended from the junction of the breasthooks; this was an amulet intended to protect the wearer from harm. The deep plated belt worn at the midriff may also be peculiar to the rank of centurion, since it is to be encountered again on the stele of the centurion Marcus Favonius Facilis (see plate E1) at Colchester.

The helmet shown on the sculpture has no transverse crest, as might have been expected, and the helmet itself is rather too stylised for the precise

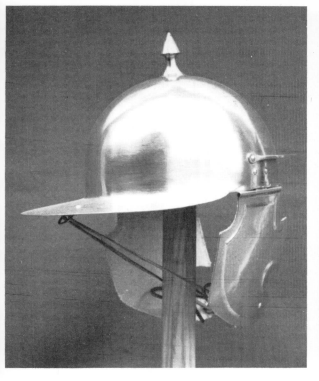

Reconstruction by the author of a Coolus type 'E' helmet of the late Augustan period. Helmets of this type appear to have been relegated to the auxiliaries as more advanced forms of armour were issued to the legions. (Riveredge Foundation, Calgary, Canada)

pattern to be identified. The helmet shown in this reconstruction is based on the remains of a bronze skull of Coolus type 'F' found in Bosham harbour and a cheek-guard found at Hod Hill in Dorset.

The *scutum* shown with the figure on the Arch of Orange displays in one corner a small 'L' shape, perhaps the earliest representation of what is thought to be a reinforcing washer for the corner of back-braces, which in turn may indicate the development of a lighter shield construction. The shield boss is of interlamination type, i.e. it was provided with a narrow flange which was set in between the laminations of the shield board during manufacture.

B2: Signifer, Legio XIV Gemina, Tiberian period

The grave stele upon which this figure is based shows a mail hauberk with a shoulder doubling more usually associated with Roman cavalry in the 1st century AD; however, mail capes had been known among the Celts in earlier periods, and the influence of Celtic armaments upon those of the

Romans is undeniable. This influence may also extend into religious practice as far as standard bearers are concerned, in connection with their now-obvious employment of what have become known as 'sports' helmets because of their association with the *Hippika Gymnasia*. The soldier also wears heavier defences of *pteruges*, both in the kilt and upper arms; again, one would expect these to have been carried by an arming doublet beneath the corselet.

The military belt carrying the dagger is also fitted with a large groin-guard or 'sporran', as it is sometimes called today. These extra defences were introduced in the early 1st century AD and were probably developed from Gallic belts with multiple terminations (see plate C2).

Resting upon the left shoulder of the figure on the grave stele is what can only be a masked helmet with a pointed diadem, bearing a very distinct resemblance to the bronze cavalry 'sports' helmet skull found at Newstead in Scotland; as already mentioned, it is most probably of significance in relation to the standard bearer's position as guardian of an object of spiritual importance. Whether or not this helmet would have been exchanged for a normal field head-piece for battle is impossible to say with any certainty; however, such legion received its formal title in AD 42 for remaining loyal to the Emperor Claudius during a revolt in Dalmatia.

The body defence of scales is called a *lorica plumata* in this instance, because the spined scales resemble feathers. The upper arm defences and kilt of *pteruges* carry fringing, a feature which appears to have been reserved for *principales* (the Senior 'NCO' grades) and above during the 1st and probably the 2nd centuries AD. An arming doublet would be used to support the *pteruges*.

The helmet and pelt drape are presumed. In Roman sculpture, eagle bearers are usually shown bare-headed; indeed, there is to date no known example of a helmeted *aquilifer*. However, even if the eagle bearer, for some religious or other reason, normally went without headgear of any kind, it might be expected that a helmet was worn in action, especially by a man who was frequently exposed to extremes of peril in battle.

The figure on the stele carries a shield on his back by means of a baldric, and though the shield is not visible it would most probably be a *parma*, a relatively small circular pattern which could be carried easily without use of the hands.

C1: Legionary infantryman, Legio VIII Augusta, mid-1st century AD.

The figure is based on the grave stele of Caius Valerius Crispus in the Stadtisches Museum, Wiesbaden (see photo of stele). The main body defences are almost identical to those of B2, except that the shoulder doubling is of the Greek cut as opposed to the 'cape'. The mail is tightly belted at the waist with a deep military belt fitted with a long groin-guard.

The sword is suspended by means of a baldric, which appeared during the first half of the 1st century AD as a replacement for one of the two elaborate belts, though the practice of wearing a sword belt did not cease completely.

The shield back shows the bracing thought to have been introduced late in the reign of Augustus. As may be seen on the original stele; the shield face bears 'L'-shaped pieces in the corners, which are probably intended to be metals, since all the painted parts of the device which would very likely have been present on the original carving have disappeared over the centuries.

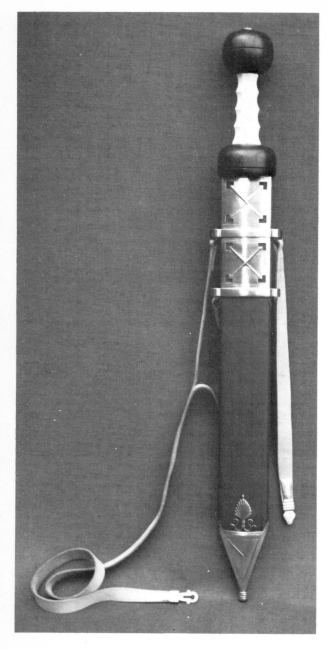

Author's reconstruction of what was probably a common issue type of 'Pompeii' pattern infantry sword, employing the scabbard mounts said to have been found at Long Windsor, Dorset, now in the Ashmolean Museum, Oxford. (Part of a complete equipment for the Hertfordshire Schools)

'sports' helmets would not have provided the best defence available.

B3: Aquilifer, Legio XI Claudia Pia Fidelis, mid-1st century AD

This figure is based on the grave stele of Lucius Sertorius Firmus in the Verona Museum, whose

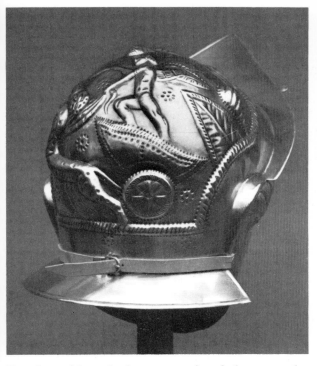

Two views of the author's reconstruction of a bronze cavalry 'sports' helmet skull of type 'B' found at Newstead near Melrose, Scotland. Helmets of this type are shown on the grave stelae of standard bearers (see colour plates). (Author's collection)

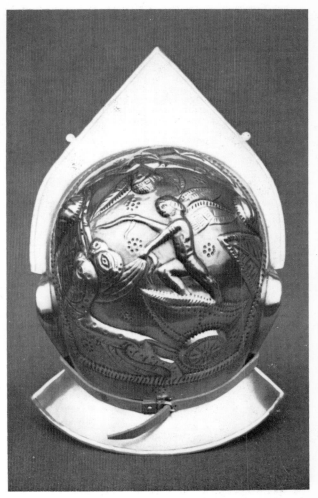

The helmet is of the type denoted Imperial Italic 'C', which is dated to the end of the second quarter and the third quarter of the 1st century AD. At this time crests would have been worn for ceremonials such as the legion's birthday celebrations, when the Eagle standard was dressed with garlands.

C2: Aquilifer, Legio XIV Gemina, first half of the 1st century AD

The figure is based on the grave stele of Gnaius Musius in the Mittelrheinisches Landesmuseum, Mainz. He is wearing what is probably a ceremonial attire, since no practical form of corselet is visible. He wears a jerkin, perhaps of hide with *pteruges* attached, over which is strapped a harness bearing his *donae*, won during his service—though the Romans did make posthumous awards.

The decorations consist of two *torques* or Celtic collars and nine *phalerae*. A further award, probably originating from Celtic spoils, is the *armilla* or bracelet worn on the right wrist. The wearing of bracelets by men was confined to the military; in civil life, the Romans considered them as purely female adornment.

The soldier also wears a military belt with the earliest form of groin-guard, the strap-end simply cut into four strips with small terminals attached, and only one strip being used to fasten the belt.

In action, Musius would probably have worn a corselet of fine mail or scale and some protection to the head, as already discussed in relation to plate B3.

C3: Centurio, Legio XI Claudia Pia Fidelis, mid-1st century AD

The figure is based on the grave stele of Quintus Sertorius Festus in the Verona Museum—possibly a contemporary relative of Lucius Sertorius Firmus. The centurion is shown in what would be ceremonial dress. He wears a scale defence with two layers of scallops to the lower edge, and single layers of *pteruges* in both the kilt and upper arm defences. Over these are his decorations consisting of nine large, elaborately embossed *phalerae* mounted on a

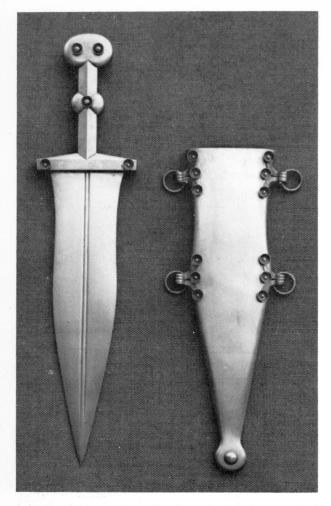

Infantry dagger and scabbard—author's reconstruction. These sidearms were usually engraved and inlaid with silver or gold and red enamel. The dagger ceases to be in evidence after the end of the 1st century AD, but re-emerges in the 3rd century as a much larger but rather poorer quality piece.

harness, two *torques*, and on his head a wreath perhaps of gilded oak leaves, a *corona civica* (the original stone is too badly damaged in this area for the wreath to be positively identified, and it may be the *corona aurea*).

The man wears a pair of embossed greaves, which were peculiar to the rank of centurion by this date. The vine staff was also symbolic of the centurionate, but had a more practical application—on the backs of the centurion's charges.

In Caesar's time it was practice to wear decorations for combat; however, it seems rather unlikely that the very beautiful *phalerae* (such as the exquisite set found near Xanten in lower Germany

and known as the Lauersfort Phalerae) would have been subjected to such treatment, unless the object of visual splendour was considered to be necessary at a particular moment.

D1: Signifer, Cohors V Asturum, 1st century AD
The figure is based on the grave stele of Pintaius in the Rheinisches Landesmuseum, Bonn. The body defence is a short mail hauberk with a band of hide at the lower edge supporting a fringe, and belted at the waist with a pair of military belts, one for each sidearm. The stele shows the belts to be arranged in a horizontal fashion, which is unusual, and may be the individual sculptor's or workshop's practice.

The pelt draping the helmet has clearly had its mask removed, a feature which can also be associated with plate D3. A possible explanation for this may be found in the non-citizen status of the unit or of the soldier concerned.

The studs on the groin-guard are not visible on the stele, and it has been assumed that here, as in other cases, these small details would have been represented in paint which has now disappeared.

D2: Auxiliary infantryman, mid-1st century AD
The figure is partly based on the stele of Annaius Daverzus, who served with the 4th Dalmatian Infantry Cohort. The figure wears the simplest type of Roman mail hauberk, with short sleeves and probably a draw-lace at the neck opening; it had a weight of approximately 14lbs.

The belts and elaborate groin-guard are based on those of Daverzus' grave stele and are, judging by archaeological finds, a suprisingly accurate sculptural representation. Daverzus himself may well have been of citizen status, since he is shown on the stele to have what is thought to be a bronze diploma, tucked into his tunic just above the belts.

The helmet is a cheap spun type, the skull having been found at Flüren and matched with a cheek-guard from Büderich. The simplicity of this piece must clearly indicate that it belonged to an auxiliary soldier, although the skull bears no inscription to attest the fact.

The soldier carries the normal auxiliary's shield, the oval *clipeus*, and a thrusting spear. A rather crude relief from the Vespasianic Praetorium at Mainz shows one of these men also carrying two light javelins as well as the spear.

D3: Imagnifer, 1st century AD

The figure is based on a cast of the grave stele of Genialis, *imagnifer* of the 7th Raetian Infantry Cohort,. in the Römisch-Germanisches Zentralmuseum, Mainz. The body defence of mail is fitted with a cape doubling over the shoulders, fastened with the normal breasthooks, and a pair of belts for the sidearms.

The stele shows the man bare-headed with his pelt and helmet resting on his left shoulder. Protruding from the pelt is the pointed diadem of a sports helmet skull with its mask removed. Comparing this feature with the *signifer* of Legio XIV Gemina (plate B2), it appears that standard bearers of non-citizen status also wore 'sports' helms for specific purposes, but had the mask removed, perhaps because of their status; the same seems to be the case with the animal pelt shown on plate D1. The imago itself was a portrait of the Emperor or a member of his family. In action, assuming the *imagnifer* became involved in the fray, he may have worn a more serviceable helmet.

E1: Centurio, Legio XX Valeria, mid-1st century AD

The figure is based on the grave stele of Marcus Favonius Facilis in the Colchester and Essex Museum, Colchester. The body defence has extensions in the deltoid region which have helped to definitely identify such corselets as mail and not leather, as many have in the past supposed. For the successful manufacture of these extensions, it is necessary to employ mailmaker's constructions which have not previously been attributed to the Romans; though why it should have been considered that the Romans were incapable of understanding one or two elementary methods of tailoring mail, which they would doubtless have learned from the Celts, is difficult to comprehend. On the stele the corselet is shown to have been edged at all three extremities, and has shoulder doubling straps which are rather longer than usual.

Experiments with the author's full-scale reconstruction, now in the Museum at Colchester, have proved that the *pteruges* must have been mounted on an arming doublet beneath the mail and were not actually attached to the corselet itself.

The greaves represented on the stele are plain, but since parts of the sculpture are known to have been finished out with gesso and would doubtless have been painted, these pieces may well have been decorated with an embossed design.

While the stele does not depict a helmet, iron head-pieces were becoming fairly widespread at the time of Facilis' death (thought to be between AD 43 and 49) and he may possibly have owned one, but he could equally well have been helmeted in bronze; at this date, a transverse crest is to be expected. To date there is no known specimen of a helmet with attachments for such a crest, but they were probably no different from those of the ordinary infantry helmets, with only the position altered.

The lack of decorations (*dona*) on this stele does show that unlike some modern armies, the Romans did not give away awards with the rations, and here is one ordinary centurion who never managed to distinguish himself. Perhaps he was a junior officer who had entered the centurionate by direct commission and died fairly young.

Auxiliary's belt and groin-guard. The buckle and belt-plates are based on pieces found at Hod Hill, Dorset, now in the Durden Collection. (Part of a complete equipment made by the author for the Corinium Museum, Cirencester)

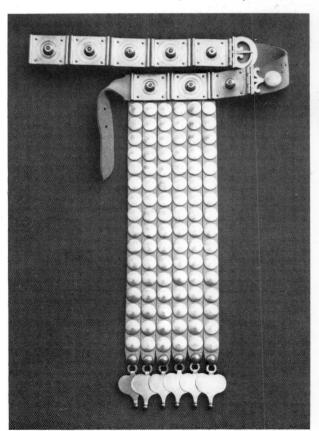

E2: Legionary infantryman, mid-1st century AD

The figure's equipment is a compilation of contemporary pieces from various sites, and is intended to represent a legionary as he might have looked late in the reign of Tiberius, when most of his equipment was developed.

The cuirass is of Corbridge type 'A', with strap fasteners between the shoulder sections and the girdles, and eight pairs of girdle plates. The helmet is of Imperial Gallic type 'E', based on a fairly well preserved skull-piece from the fort at Valkenburg, Holland. The fittings of the sword scabbard are reconstructed from the remains said to have been found at Long Windsor, Dorset; they were probably found originally on the site of the fort at Waddon Hill in the same county, and are now in the Ashmolean Museum. The javelin is of the type from the fort at Oberaden in Germany, where three good specimens of this 1st-century weapon were found. The method of covering and carrying the shield

Reconstruction of the *vexillum* said to have been found in a grave in Egypt, the original flag now in the Museum of Fine Arts, Moscow. The side pendant terminals are based on an example found in the streambed of the Walbrook, London.

seems to have remained the same, and it might be expected that many a damaged shoulder-splint hinge was caused by this practice.

E3: Legionary infantryman, second half of the 1st century AD

The equipment shown on this figure is again compiled from various sources, and represents a legionary from the late second quarter onward.

The cuirass is of Corbridge type 'B', which had hook and loop connectors between the shoulder sections and girdles, and only seven pairs of girdle plates instead of eight. It is possible that this type of cuirass was in manufacture and being issued by the early AD 40s, since a plate from a hinged shoulder-splint conforming very much more closely to the pattern of 'B' type was quite recently excavated from the site of the invasion supply base of Legio II Augusta at Chichester, which was occupied during the first five years of the invasion of Britain. The plate in question shows no signs of ever having been fitted to a cuirass.

The javelin is a new type with a large lead weight to increase the weapon's degree of penetration, a feature which continues into the late Empire, until the heavy javelin disappeared altogether. The helmet is of Imperial Gallic type 'F', based on the virtually complete example from the amphitheatre at Besançon, now in the Besançon Museum. The mounts on the sword scabbard are from Germany, but are of a very similar type to those found with the remains of three swords on the site of Pompeii, from which site these swords have gained their modern name.

F1: Legionary infantryman, Legio II Adiutrix, late 1st century AD

The figure is based on the grave stele of Caius Castricius in the Aquincum Museum, Budapest. The body defences appear to be very like those of the earlier years of the 1st century AD, and may provide us with a vivid example of the Roman policy of issuing equipment in a serviceable condition regardless of its age. However, the practice of doubling up the thickness of mail on the shoulders, for both infantry and cavalry, has ceased; it was probably regarded as unnecessary extra weight, of which any reduction would have been welcomed by the infantry, no doubt.

The stele shows the soldier wearing his helmet with cresting of both a horse-hair brush and side-plumes, though the forepart of the helmet has been retracted to expose the entire face and some of the man's hair. The helmet used in the reconstruction is of Imperial Gallic type 'I', recovered from the River Rhine at Mainz (see author's reconstruction). The original helmet belonged to a legionary serving with Legio I Adiutrix, a legion raised at the same date as that of Castricius.

Another unusual piece of equipment displayed on the stele is an oval shield with a boss clearly worked to represent a face, probably the Gorgon Medusa. A remarkably similar boss was found in Holland and is now in the Rijksmuseum G.M. Kam, Nijmegen; it has been copied for this colour plate.

Whether or not sword baldrics were frequently studded in the manner shown is impossible to tell; however, the stele of Castricius shows this in clear detail, but as usual omits the baldric fastener. Others may, of course, have been represented in paint and since lost.

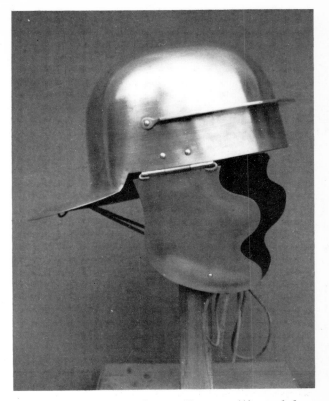

Author's reconstruction of an auxiliary type 'A' spun helmet based on the original bronze skull in the Rheinisches Landesmuseum, Bonn, with cheek-guards of Büderich type. (Corinium Museum, Cirencester)

F2: Auxiliary infantryman of a Cohors Equitata, Trajanic period

This soldier was almost the lowest rank in the Roman army. His body defence is a simple mail hauberk which could be either plain, or 'dagged' as shown at its extremities. His legs are protected from the cold by what were probably called *bracae*, the long trousers which the Romans normally associated with the barbarian nations, giving rise to the derogatory term *bracati*. He is wearing *perones* on his feet, which are a more suitable form of footwear for cold climates, and it may be considered that these were much more widely used than appears to be the case by a mere survey of sculptural representations.

The helmet, of Auxiliary Infantry type 'C', was simple but very sturdy, and of warlike appearance in its coldly efficient design. The reconstruction is based on the skull-piece in the Museo Archaeologico, Florence, which has had its neck-guard and part of the nape cut away at a later date and a series of holes punched all the way round the base of the skull for the attachment of a lining; the latter is clearly not Roman work, since they always glued their linings in position. Many helmets of this kind may be seen in stylised form on Trajan's Column.

His sword would obviously be of the cheapest variety available, probably with an all-wooden hilt and very basic scabbard mounts and baldric fastener, such as the specimen found at Newstead in Scotland.

F3: Legionary infantryman, Trajanic period

The equipment shown on this figure is mainly based on finds from two sites: the cuirass plates from Newstead in Scotland, and the helmet from Brigetio on the Danube, near Budapest. The cuirass is considerably altered by this date. Gone are all the hinges and buckle fasteners, and the primary shoulder-guard splint is now a single plate instead of three. The collar is made from a total of six plates and has a larger, more comfortable neck-opening. The collar halves are fastened together by loops and pins which prevent any movement of the collar opening. There appears to have been a fourth type of cuirass, with laminations extending all the way up to the neck, front and rear; however, the evidence is as yet purely sculptural and finds are awaited to prove the method of construction.

The groin-guard is only half the length of the earlier type (Trajan's Column) and the dagger seems to have been made obsolete.

The helmet from the Brigetio fort, denoted Imperial Gallic type 'J', the remains of which are in the possession of the Tower of London, has a good deep neck-guard and a well-formed skull, with a peak which is angled slightly upward. The cheek-guards were of an angular pattern almost identical to a specimen found at Chester, England. So alike are they that the equipment must have originated from the same workshop.

G1: Provincial legate, early Imperial period
The figure is based on relatively common sculptures of the period, of which there must originally have been a vast number produced for circulation throughout the Empire, many of which would have been destroyed when a particular individual fell from grace. These works usually show *pteruges* employed in double layers at the deltoids and sometimes a triple layer for the 'kilt', one layer being very much shorter than the other two. These were presumably attached to an arming doublet. Over this would be worn either a short muscle cuirass (of the type portrayed) if the man was to be mounted on a horse, or one of infantry type which had an abdominal extension, usually with a row of decorated lappets protruding below the corselet. The embossed figures and designs on the armour were either raised out of the plate, or sometimes applied pieces attached with small rivets. The helmet is an example, from Autun in France, of what must surely be a senior officer's parade helmet; it was certainly not intended for use in combat. The neck-guard is laminated and has three internal leathers.

G2: Junior tribune, early Imperial period
This officer's rank is determined by the narrow stripe on his tunic, which meant that he was of Equestrian status (*tribunus augusticlavius*). There were five of these officers serving with a legion, and one senior tribune (*tribunus laticlavius*) who wore a broad stripe to signify that he was about to enter the Senate.

The figure wears knee breeches which were probably called *feminalia*, a word derived from *femen*—the lesser-known Latin word for the thigh. These garments are seen to be common to *principales* and all higher ranks, and to all the auxiliaries, both horse and foot, on Trajan's Column, but are not worn by the legionary infantry; precisely why remains an open question. No doubt the muscle cuirass worn by this officer would have been less ornate than that of the legate, especially in parade equipment, though the tribunes also wore a knotted sash around the corselet as a symbol of rank.

The helmet is hypothetical, based on an embossed representation. The brow-plate, however, is copied from an example in the Rijks-museum, Leiden. Such helmets of Attic form are frequently portrayed in Roman sculpture and clearly did exist; however, a reasonably complete specimen has yet to be discovered.

G3: Cornicen, Trajanic period
The figure is based on representations of horn-players on Trajan's Column. The soldier wears a *lorica squamata* of quite fine scale, worked into lappets at its extremities and edged with hide. The scales were probably stitched to a foundation of coarse linen, similar to a recently discovered portion of a Severan scale corselet from Carpow, Scotland, which is backed with two-over-one linen twill. The helmet is of Imperial Italic type 'G', after the specimen said to have been found in a cave at Hebron, Israel. The original helmet is now in the Israel Museum, Jerusalem. The *cornu* itself was a very old instrument, perhaps of Etruscan origin. The Roman version probably had a high-pitched sound, in order that it could be heard above the din of battle. The *cornu* was also used in civil life; a mosaic at Nennig, District of Saarburg, shows a *cornu* being played in conjunction with an organ as accompaniment to gladiatorial combat.

H1: Cavalry trooper, Ala Noricum, second half of the 1st century AD
The figure is based on the grave stele of Titus

Reconstruction by the author of a 'Pompeii' pattern infantry sword and scabbard. Weapons of this type appeared during the first half of the 1st century AD, certainly prior to the invasion of Britain. Elaborate decoration of this kind was apparently common, though there was a simpler type represented by the Long Windsor fragments. (Part of a complete equipment now in the Rijksmuseum G.M. Kam, Nijmegen, Netherlands)

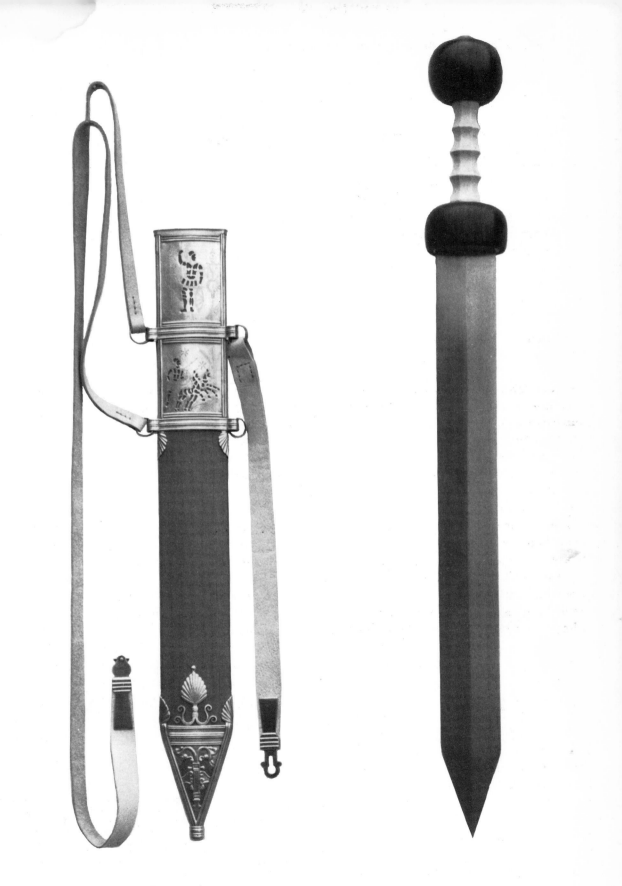

Flavius Bassus, who served in the *turma* of Fabius Pudens in the Flavian period. The stele was found at Cologne and is now in the Römisch-Germanisches Museum, Cologne. The trooper is shown wearing the common mail hauberk without sleeves and with a doubling cape. The mail has short slits at the sides to allow greater comfort in the saddle. The helmet is based on a fragmentary specimen found at Koblenz-Bubenheim, and probably represents the second stage of the development of Roman cavalry head-pieces. The large, flat, projecting peak is peculiar to the cavalry, as are cheek-guards with embossed ears which fit into the ear recesses in the helmet's skull-piece. All the helmets of this class are iron helmets primarily, decorated with thin embossed bronze skinning; part of the skinning was silvered as shown. The soldier wears *feminalia*, which appear to have been common to all cavalrymen of the 1st century and later. He also wears the same pattern of boots as the infantry, with the addition of simple prick-spurs.

The main weapon of the cavalryman was the thrusting-spear, which could be used couched as a lance, wielded over-arm to stab, or quite possibly thrown at adversaries, the rider then returning to his own lines to be replenished by his attendant (who is often portrayed in the rear of the trooper on grave stelae, carrying two or more spears). The cavalry sword of this date was not a particularly weighty weapon, rather to be regarded as a back-up to the spears. Apart from its greater length of blade this *spatha* is essentially similar to the infantry sword.

The harness of the cavalry ponies was obviously quite heavily decorated with ornaments, since a very large quantity of these fittings have been found on many of the sites where cavalry units had been present. It may be expected that the cavalry *alae* were more smartly fitted out than the equestrian section of a *cohors equitata*.

H2: Cavalry trooper, Ala Noricum, mid-1st century AD
The figure is based on the grave stele of Caius Romanius, who served in the *turma* of Claudius Capito. The stele may be seen in the Mittelrheinisches Landesmuseum, Mainz. While the stele provides no clue as to whether the body defence of this man was mail or scale armour, the use of scale by the cavalry appears to have been fairly common, and this type of armour could just as easily have been painted onto the sculpture as would have been the case with a representation of mail.

The helmet is based on fragments from various locations, largely the lower Rhine area. It is clear from the finds that a large proportion of cavalry head-pieces of this date were not fitted with a peak such as that shown on the Koblenz specimen. The Witcham Gravel helmet in the collection of the

A gate and section of turf and timber rampart reconstructed in its original position at the Lunt Fort, Baginton, near Coventry. The original fort was built shortly after the Boudican Revolt of AD 60–61, and may be a training base for cavalry mounts.

Two views of the author's hypothetical reconstruction of a mid-1st century cavalry trooper's helmet, based on fragments from Nijmegen and Leiden. The helmet has an iron skull and cheek-guards, skinned with embossed bronze. (Author's collection)

...ritish Museum is a reasonably well preserved ...ample of one of these. Though it is difficult to ...tablish with certainty at this time, it appears that ...e peakless helms were slightly earlier in date than ...eir peaked equivalents. It is certain, however, ...at almost all of the surviving helmets from the end ...the 1st century onward were fitted with peaks of ...e form or another, with the exception of some ...ep bronze helms which were of the lowest order.

The pony's harness bears small cast bronze ...ecorations along the breech and breastbands; ...ese objects, a considerable number of which ...rvive, have often been incorrectly identified as ...tings from infantry groin-guards—or, to use ...rchaeological parlance, 'apron terminals'. Judging ...y the height of several surviving bronze saddlehorn ...iffener plates and the remains of saddle leathers, it ...ppears that Roman saddles were fitted with a ...irly thick cushion and would certainly have ...quired a pair of girths.

Bibliography, and author's address

H. R. Robinson: *The Armour of Imperial Rome* (1975)
G. Webster: *The Roman Imperial Army* (1969)
Peter Connolly: *Greece and Rome at War* (1981)
Peter Connolly: *The Roman Army* (1975)
Robert F. Evans: *Legions of Imperial Rome—An Informal Order of Battle Study* (1980)
V. A. Maxfield: *The Military Decorations of the Roman Army* (1981)
Polybius: *The Histories*—Loeb (1967)

Readers interested in obtaining further information about **reconstructed Roman military equipment** may contact the author through the following address: 9a Priory Road, West Bridgford, Nottingham NG2 5HU, England.

Notes sur les planches en couleur

A1 Cette cotte de mailles a été copiée d'après l'autel de *Domitius Ahenobarbus* au Louvre. Le casque est un type 'C' *Montefortino*. Le bouclier est un modèle primitif de *scutum* conçu d'après le bouclier celtique plat de forme similaire, cependant celui-ci est maintenant en bois contre-plaqué—changement de matériau rendu nécessaire par la nouvelle courbure. L'armure de corps copiée d'après l'Arche d'Orange, datant de l'époque de Tibère; la cotte est maintenant munie de *pteruges* supplémentaires en cuir qui sont ajoutés aux bras et aux cuisses. Le casque est de type 'C' *Coolus* et a été reproduit d'après un exemple du Liechtenstein. Le haut et le bas du *scutum* ont été coupés et commence à évoluer vers le type plus tardif de forme semi-cylindrique. **A3** La chemise de mailles plus longue, à nouveau copiée d'après l'Arche d'Orange, élimine le besoin de *pteruges* aux cuisses. Le casque est du type 'E' *Coolus* et est tiré de l'exemple de Walbrook. Le bouclier est couvert pour une marche sur territoire ami; il est rejeté en arrière sur une sangle et laisse la main libre pour tenir le bâton à bagage.

B1 Cet exemple est tiré en partie de l'Arche d'Orange et en partie de la tombe de *M. Favonius Facilis*; le casque est du type 'F' *Coolus*. A noter les coins en 'L' renforcés du bouclier. **B2** Cet exemple est tiré d'une tombe. On pense maintenant que les casques à visière nommés autrefois 'casques de sports de la cavalerie' ont aussi été portés par les portes-étendard de l'infanterie. **B3** Reproduction d'après la tombe de *L. Sertorius Firmus*. La *lorica plumata*, le petit bouclier rond *parma*, et les *pteruges* aux extrémités à franges semblent tous être associés aux *principales*: ce que l'on pourrait appeler les rangs 'sous-officiers'.

C1 Cet exemple est basé en grande partie sur la tombe de *C. Valerius Crispus*. Noter le baudrier séparé de l'épée, la main protège-aine tombant de la ceinture du poignard ainsi que le casque de type 'C' Impérial Italique, orné d'un cimier pour une cérémonie quelconque. **C2** Exemple pris d'après la tombe de *Gn. Musius*, il porte ce qui semble être un uniforme de cérémonie avec décorations complètes et sans armure. **C3** Copié d'après la tombe de *Q. Sertorius Festus*, ce centurion porte un habit de cérémonie, avec corselet d'armure en écailles, décorations complètes et couronne de la *corona civica*. Noter les jambarts, particuliers aux centurions de cette époque, et le bâton de vigne, marque de son rang.

D1 D'après la tombe de *Pintaeus*; noter les détails de la chemise de mailles. La tête de la peau d'animal portée sur les épaules et le casque a été coupée, ce qui semblerait indiquer que cette unité appartenait aux *Auxilia*. **D2** Reproduction tirée en partie de la tombe d'*Annaius Daverzus* de la 4ème Cohort de l'infanterie dalmate. Cet équipement et cette armure sont des exemples typiques de ceux des troupes *Auxilia* à tous égards. Ils sont bon marché, simples et plutôt démodés. Le bouclier *clipeus* ovale et la lance sont caractéristiques. **D3** Basé sur la tombe de *Genialis*, *imagnifer* de la 7ème Cohort d'infanterie raétienne, et montrant la peau d'animal dont la tête a été ôtée, et le diadème à pointe de ce qui semble être ce que l'on nomme un casque de 'sports'.

E1 D'après la tombe de *M. Favonius Facilis*. On peut supposer qu'il s'agit d'un casque en fer ou en bronze, avec cimier transversal, à été coupé. **E2** Une représentation construite d'après différentes découvertes archéologiques; la *lorica segmentata* primitive est du type classé *Corbridge* modèle 'A', le casque du type Gaulois Impérial modèle 'E'. **E3** Autre reconstruction de modèle plus récent—la cuirasse est maintenant du type *Corbridge* modèle 'B', le casque est du type Gaulois Impérial modèle 'F', et la pointe de javelot est allourdie.

F1 D'après le tombe de *C. Castricius*. Bien que ce costume soit de la fin du 1er siècle AD, il comporte de nombreuses caractéristiques associés à ceux des années du début du siècle. Ceci nous rappelle que les nouveaux modèles d'armures et d'équipements n'ont pas remplacé uniformément dans tout l'empire les anciens modèles, et que notre connaissance en matière de 'temps' est très superficielle. **F2** Un soldat de rang et d'unité inférieurs portant un costume simple avec pantalons et bottes ajoutées pour temps froid. **F3** La cuirasse est beaucoup plus simple maintenant et a une forme moins décorée; le protège-aine est beaucoup plus court, le casque est du type Gaulois Impérial modèle 'J'.

G1 Les caractéristiques générales du costume d'officier supérieur sont connues d'après les nombreuses sculptures et comprennent typiquement une 'cuirasse musculaire', comme celle-ci, et plusieurs rangées de *pteruges*. Ce casque étonnant, trouvé à Autun en France, a certainement appartenu à un officier supérieur, sa forme et sa richesse laissent présumer qu'il s'agissait d'un casque de parade plutôt que de combat. **G2** La bande mince pourpre sur la tunique identifie le *tribunus augusticlavius*, officier d'état-major, dont il y en avait cinq par légion. Le casque est de forme attique, apparemment caractéristique des rangs supérieurs. **G3** Ce costume de trompettiste est tiré de la Colonne Trajane et de trouvailles en Israel et en Ecosse.

H1 Exemple d'après la tombe de *T. Flavius Bassus*. Le casque avec 'oreillettes' en relief et visière large et plate est caractéristique aux hommes de la cavalerie auxiliaire, ainsi que la combinaison de chemise de mailles et des pantalons courts en cuir, la lance, et le bouclier ovale et plat. **H2** En partie d'après la tombe de *C. Romanius*. Les armures d'écailles étaient aussi souvent utilisées que les cottes de mailles si l'on en juge par les sculptures ayant survécu, c'est pourquoi nous avons choisi d'en présenter une ici en contraste avec H1.

Farbtafeln

A1 Dieser Panzer ist nach dem Altar des *Domitius Ahenobarbus* im Louvr entworfen. Der Helm ist ein *Montefortino* Typ 'C'. Der Schild ist ein frühes *scutu* eine Entwicklung des flachen keltischen Schilds, der eine ähnliche Form hatt dieses Exemplar ist jedoch aus Sperrholz; ein Material, das durch die Krümm notwendig wurde. **A2** Eine vom Triumphbogen in *Orange* kopierte Rüstung a der tiberianischen Zeit; der Panzer hat zusätzliche lederne *pteruges* an Armen un Schenkeln. Der Helm ist ein Coolus Typ 'C', einem Exemplar in Liechtenste nachempfunden. Beim *scutum* sind Ober- und Unterseite beschnitten; die For nähert sich dem späteren halb-zylindrischen Typ. **A3** Bei diesem lange Kettenhemd (ebenfalls nach dem Triumphbogen von *Orange* entworfen) sind d *pteruges* an den Oberschenkeln überflüssig. Der Helm, basierend auf der Walbrook-Exemplar, ist ein *Coolus* Typ 'E'. Der Schild ist für einen Marsch d Territorium eines befreundeten Landes bedeckt; er wird an einem Riem getragen, so dass die Hand für die Gepäckstange frei bleibt.

B1 Der Helm, ein *Coolus* Typ 'F', basiert teils auf dem Triumphbogen von *Orang* teils auf dem Grabstein des *M. Favonius Facilis*. Man beachte die L-förmig Verstärkungen an den Schildecken. **B2** Ein Entwurf nach einem Grabstein. M wird heute angenommen, dass die früher als 'Kavallerie-Sporthelm bezeichneten Kopfbedeckungen auch von Standartenträgern der Infanter getragen wurden. **B3** Ein Entwurf nach dem Grabstein des *L. Sertorius Firmus*. Di *lorica plumata*, der kleine runde *parma*-Schild und die *pteruges* mit gefranste Rändern verweisen auf die *principales*, die wir heute als führende Unteroffizie bezeichnen könnten.

C1 In erster Linie nach dem Grabstein des *C. Valerius Crispus* entworfen. Ma beachte das separate Schwertgehenk, den Leistenschutz unter dem Dolchgürt und den Helm vom kaiserlich-italischen Typ 'C', hier für eine Zeremon geschmückt. **C2** Offenbar eine zeremonielle Uniform mit vollen Dekoratione und ohne Waffen, basierend auf dem Grabstein des *Gn. Musius*. **C3** Dieser nac dem Grabstein des *Q. Sertorius Festus* entworfene Centurion trägt zeremoniel Bekleidung mit Schuppenpanzer-Harnisch, vollen Dekorationen und dem Kra der *corona civica*. Man beachte die für den Centurion bezeichnenden Beinschien und die Weinrebe, sein Rangabzeichen.

D1 Vom Grabstein des *Pintaeus*; man beachte die Details des Kettenhemds. D dem über Schulter und Helm getragenen Tierfell wurde das Gesic abgeschnitten, eventuel ein Hinweis auf die *Auxilia* Rolle dieser Einheit. **D2** Z Teil nach dem Grabstein des *Annaius Daverzus* der 4. dalmatinische Infanterie *Cohort* gezeichnet. Ausrüstung und Rüstung sind für die *auxili* Truppen typisch: sie sind billig, einfach und recht altmodisch. Der ovale *clipe* Schild und der Wurfspeer sind ebenfalls charakteristisch. **D3** Ein Entwurf nac dem Grabstein des *Genialis*, *imagnifer* der 7. rätischen Infanterie *Cohort*, m gesichtslosem Tierfell und dem spitzen Diadem des sogenannten Sport-Helm

E1 Vom Grabstein des *M. Favonius Facilis*. Zu dieser Zeit kann ein eiserner od bronzener Helm mit diagonalem Helmbusch angenommen werden. **E2** Ei nach verschiedenen archäologischen Funden rekonstruierte Figur; die frühe *lori segmentata* ist als *Corbridge* 'A' klassifiziert, der Helm als kaiserlich-gallischer Ty 'E'. **E3** Eine spätere Rekonstruktion—der Kürass ist diesmal ein *Corbridge* Ty 'B', der Helm in kaiserlich-gallischer Typ 'F' und der Wurfspiess hat ei schwere Spitze für besonders grosse Durchschlagskraft.

F1 Vom Grabstein des *C. Castricius*. Obwohl, das Kostüm aus dem späten 1. Jh. Chr. stammt, weist es viele Züge auf, die wir mit den Anfängen dies Jahrhunderts verbinden. Es zeigt sich wiederum, dass neue Rüstungs- un Waffentypen die alten nicht systematisch in allen Teilen des Kaiserreic ersetzten, und dass wir nur wenig über den 'Zeitplan' wissen. **F2** Ein Sold niederen Ranges von einer unteren Einheit in einem einfachen Kostüm m Hosen und Stiefeln für kaltes Wetter. **F3** Der Kürass ist jetzt viel einfacher u weniger dekoriert, der Leistenschutz ist viel kürzer, und der Helm ist e kaiserlich-gallischer Typ 'J'.

G1 Die Kennzeichen des Kostüms eines leitenden Offiziers sind von viele Plastiken her bekannt. Dazu gehört häufig ein 'Muskel-Kürass' wie dieser he ausserdem mehrere Reihen von *pteruges*. Dieser ungewöhnliche, in Autu (Frankreich) gefundene Helm hat sicher einem leitenden Offizier gehört; sei und reiche Dekoration verweisen auf einen Paradehelm. **G2** Der schmal purpurne Streifen auf der Tunika verweist auf *tribunus augusticlavius*, v denen in jeder Legion fünf Vertreter als Stabsoffiziere dienten. Der Helm attische Form, offenbar typisch für höhere Ränge. **G3** Dieses Kostüm ei Trompeters ist von der Trajanssäule übernommen sowie aus Funden in Isra und Schottland.

H1 Nach dem Grabstein des *T. Flavius Bassus*. Charakteristisch für d Kavallerie-Hilfstruppen sind der Helm mit bossierten 'Ohren' und einem flach Oberteil, die Kombination von Kettenhemd und kurzen Leder-Kniehosen un der Speer und der flache ovale Schild. **H2** Zum Teil nach dem Grabstein des *Romanius*. Schuppenpanzer wurden ebenso häufig wie Kettenpanzer benutzt, w aus den erhaltenen Bildwerken hervorgeht; dieses Beispiel ist als Kontrast zu H abgebildet.

MEN-AT-ARMS SERIES

EDITOR: MARTIN WINDROW

The Roman Army from Caesar to Trajan

Text by MICHAEL SIMKINS

Colour plates by RONALD EMBLETON

OSPREY PUBLISHING LONDON

Published in 1984 by
Osprey Publishing Ltd
59 Grosvenor Street, London W1X 9DA
© Copyright 1984 Osprey Publishing Ltd
Reprinted 1985 (twice), 1986, 1987, 1988 (three times)

British Library Cataloguing in Publication Data

Simkins, Michael
    The Roman Army from Caesar to Trajan. [*Rev. ed.*]
    —(Men-at-Arms series; 46)
    1. Rome—Army—History
    I. Title   II. Series
    355'.00937   U35

    ISBN 0-85045-528-6

Filmset in Great Britain
Printed in Hong Kong

Editor's note
This book is a revised and entirely
re-illustrated treatment of the edition
first published under the same title
and MAA series number in 1974.